Food Presentation

Tips & Inspiration

Schiffer® Publishing Ltd

880 Lower Valley Road, Atglen, PA 19310

Michelle Valigursky

Photographic Assistance by Nicholas Valigursky

Other Schiffer Books by the Author:
Creating Curb Appeal, 978-0-7643-3278-4, $24.99

Other Schiffer Books on Related Subjects:
Table Decor, 978-0-7643-2472-1, $24.95
Table Decoration with Fruits and Vegetables, 978-0-7643-3510-5, $24.99
Cakes for All Occasions, 978-0-7643-2904-3, $24.95
Sugar Art, 978-0-7643-3382-8, $24.99
Entertaining with Flowers, 978-0-7643-2556-6, $29.95
Creating Floral Centerpieces, 978-0-7643-3459-7, $29.99

Library of Congress Control Number: 2010925030

Designed by John P. Cheek
Cover design by Bruce Waters
Type set in Coronet/DeVinne BT/Zurich Lt BT

ISBN: 978-0-7643-3481-8
Printed in China

Schiffer Books are available at special discounts for bulk purchases for sales promotions or premiums. Special editions, including personalized covers, corporate imprints, and excerpts can be created in large quantities for special needs. For more information contact the publisher:

Published by Schiffer Publishing Ltd.
4880 Lower Valley Road
Atglen, PA 19310
Phone: (610) 593-1777; Fax: (610) 593-2002
E-mail: Info@schifferbooks.com

For the largest selection of fine reference books on this and related subjects, please visit our web site at
www.schifferbooks.com
We are always looking for people to write books on new and related subjects. If you have an idea for a book please contact us at the above address.

This book may be purchased from the publisher.
Include $5.00 for shipping.
Please try your bookstore first.
You may write for a free catalog.

In Europe, Schiffer books are distributed by
Bushwood Books
6 Marksbury Ave.
Kew Gardens
Surrey TW9 4JF England
Phone: 44 (0) 20 8392 8585; Fax: 44 (0) 20 8392 9876
E-mail: info@bushwoodbooks.co.uk
Website: www.bushwoodbooks.co.uk

Dedication

This book is dedicated to mom and dad, the first culinary champions in my life to inspire my love of great food and exotic flavors. You set the example for how to throw a party everyone wanted to attend. I love you both very much.

Acknowledgments

I've always appreciated the beauty of food, and exploring its tastes and textures and artistic qualities for presentation has been a complete joy.

This wouldn't have been possible without the continued enthusiasm, support, and healthy appetites of my amazing family and friends, who enjoyed all the food you see photographed here. This book chronicles a large part of our lives over many months, capturing in photos the great parties, great food, and great company we've been so privileged to enjoy.

Ed – my love and my very best friend. Thank you for believing in me all these years. And thank you even more for putting up with the chaos of a kitchen photo studio and cries of "you can't eat that until I take the picture!" You're a very patient man, and I love you, always and forever. You will always warm my heart and make me smile. And don't forget . . . this culinary journey of ours started with that first late night of steak and fettuccine more than thirty years ago. . .

Nicholas – my photo assistant. You are a talented, incredible son. This book would not have been possible without your help and hard work. Thank you for understanding my creative vision and putting up with my perfectionism.

Michael – my technical guru and loyal supporter. I appreciate that you're always ready and willing to ease me through the glitches in my life, no matter what they may be. You are my life's gift and I intend to teach you to cook and present your own food beautifully now that you're out on your own!

Mom. You were the original "***hostess with the mostest***" and you set the example. I appreciate your many talents, and your willingness to share your beautiful things to make this book lovelier.

Dad and Pat. Thank you for cheering me on, sharing meals, sharing recipes, and sharing pictures of your beautiful pies!

Lori and Scott, Susan and Brad, Earlene and Jeff, Jan and Bob. You were my dining companions, my last minute set-up helpers, and loyal supporters. You're the best!

Maddie, Daniel, Trent, and Jay – my golden spoon club. Who could ask for better tasters or a better niece and nephews?

Dee and Ed – You are great friends with a great spirit. And your garden retreat is one of my favorite spots on earth. I'm glad we continue to share amazing meals and conversations in each other's company.

This book journey, too, has included "prop shopping" day and night. With hundreds of photos in the planning stages at any one time, I've been on a constant quest for the perfect plate or serving platter to highlight specific foods or techniques. My friends and family have come through for me, loaning me precious heirlooms to photograph to give you the widest array of presentation styles possible.

I'd also like to thank Tina Skinner, Jesse Marth, John Cheek, Bruce Waters, and Douglas Congdon-Martin at Schiffer Publishing for understanding my vision.

May your food, and your lives, be truly beautiful!

Michelle Valigursky

Contents

Tools of the Trade

Serve balled fresh melon in stemless martini glasses for an elegant presentation.

Dinner and a Show

We all love a great show, don't we? Cue up the music and lights, add drama and action, roll curtain and let the big show begin. That's what a great meal is like: part ambience, part showmanship, part emotional satisfaction. Mix it all together and you've got a recipe for mealtime success.

To entertain well is to share a part of yourself with family and friends. We give from our spirits around the dinner table or at the buffet, sharing conversation and the simple pleasures of food prepared well. When food is presented beautifully, enjoyment is enhanced and guests walk away feeling satisfied on many levels.

Shift your paradigm and begin to think of food as the raw material for an artistic creation. There are no hard and fast rules – just colors and textures and dimension. The plate becomes your canvas for creation. Much like a graphic designer or artist considers how to place color on a blank canvas, restaurant chefs rely on truly simple presentation techniques designed to impress. Saucing, sculpting, elevating, and compartmentalizing foods are the tricks of the trade to be called upon when assembling a dinner plate or serving platter.

"Drama is very important in life: You have to come on with a bang. You never want to go out with a whimper."

— Julia Child

Dinner goes fresh with al dente pasta, extra virgin olive oil, halved grape tomatoes, and sweet basil cut into long thin strips. This knife technique is called chiffonade. To make the chiffonade, stack clean basil leaves, roll them, and cut through layers into thin strips using a chef's knife. Toss leafy strips with pasta for a lovely contrast in color and texture. Keep a wedge of Parmesan Reggiano on hand for each guest to grate tableside using the microplane.

Stenciling balsamic glaze onto a crisp, white plate offers a creative "salad" presentation for succulent summer berries. Consider purchasing a variety of small, plastic stencils to use in food presentation. This same technique works beautifully for adding just a taste of frosting or thick sauces. For more information on how to use stencils in dessert presentations, refer to page 18.

Some fruits and vegetables come ready-made for presenting food beautifully. Thin slices of carambola – or star fruit – offer a wow-power garnish for drinks, salads and fruit plates.

After you've been introduced to these techniques through hundreds of photographs, you need to begin experimenting with your very next meal. The best part? Beautiful presentation often doesn't take any longer than just dropping food on the plate. Make presenting food beautifully a conscious habit and change your home dining experience forever.

My Philosophy

Many years ago, as a newlywed with a baby, I learned an important lesson that shaped the way I think about food and entertaining. It doesn't matter how much money you have to entertain well. It's about sharing with friends and family, keeping spirits light, and having a good time.

Food doesn't have to be complicated to be enjoyed. Of course, that's not to say that I don't love to push myself to create deluxe recipes and menus for special occasions and celebrations. I do. But as a rule, I try to keep foods simple, and I always use the freshest ingredients available.

If food looks beautiful on the plate or table, people will relax and enjoy it. Small bowls of olives or toasted nuts scattered throughout a cocktail party can be just as satisfying as a country pate that takes hours to make. A simple cutting board of sliced grilled meats, a loaf of crusty bread, and a great bottle of wine at the kitchen counter may even be enjoyed more than a complex chateaubriand with duxelles in puff pastry beneath the chandelier in the formal dining room.

Fuss less, make the food you serve pretty, and the cook and guests all can enjoy the meal together.

My dinner companions never quite know what to expect when they arrive for a meal at my home. We could be honoring the bounty of a summer farmer's market, sampling cured meats from the local butcher, or tasting handmade artisan pastas from the Italian gourmet shop around the corner. I'm always on a quest for new flavors, and I regularly try foods new to me.

Since themes are so much fun to explore, I use all the spaces in my home to entertain. I've set up a dinner reflective of the American

Dress up an after school snack with a cool glass, a beautiful plate, and a neat stack of fresh-from-the-oven chocolate chip cookies. Presenting food beautifully is about making individual dining moments special and memorable.

For the most vibrant and delicious food, always shop "in season."

"A white truffle, which elsewhere might sell for hundreds of dollars, seemed easier to come by than something fresh and green. What could be got from the woods was free and amounted to a diurnal dining diary that everyone kept in their heads. May was wild asparagus, arugula, and artichokes. June was wild lettuce and stinging nettles. July was cherries and wild strawberries. August was forest berries. September was porcini."

— Bill Buford

Northwest, scotch tastings reminiscent of the Scottish moors, glittering holiday parties with sumptuous buffets, and kids' festivities with all the bells and whistles and sticky treats. My ideas are endless, and inspiration is everywhere.

If I can teach each of you something, it is this:

- Use great ingredients
- Be creative
- Play with your food to make it pretty

Welcome to my kitchen! Now let's have some fun and learn how to present food beautifully!

Michelle Valigursky

Picture Glossary of Tools to Use

Tools make the job easy. Ask any handyman trying to build a deck without his electric drill, saw, or hammer, and you'll find someone disgruntled with the job. Presenting food beautifully, while not essentially complicated, is made infinitely easier if the right tools are at hand.

So what are those tools? Begin with the basic requirements for every kitchen: good knives.

Knives

Every home cook should have a basic assortment of professional-quality knives, made to last and able to maintain a sharp edge. Blades should be made of high nickel steel to prevent rusting. For maximum durability, handles should be crafted from anti-bacterial polymer and blades should be embedded full-tang. A full tang knife uses a solid piece of shaped steel from tip to tip, surrounded and encased by handle material below the cutting blade. This adds stability and durability to the knife. For half-tang knives, blade length stops just an inch or so below the top portion of the handle. These knives are generally less expensive than full-tang knives and are less durable in the long run. Wooden handles, while rustic and decorative, pose challenges for sanitation and durability.

Knives are an investment item, so consider your purchases wisely. Do your homework and price shop. Understand guarantees for each product. Sometimes spending a little more up front to invest in a guaranteed, well-crafted knife pays off. Inexpensive knives that dull quickly or break lose their appeal and force the cook to purchase new ones time and time again.

To accomplish most kitchen tasks, a good knife set should include:

- paring knife
- boning knife
- 8-inch chef's knife with large blade
- serrated-edge bread knife
- steak knives

Every home cook will find his or her comfort zone when it comes to knives. Perhaps the 4-inch paring knife with the comfort-grip handle will suit your hand better than the 5-inch parer with the straight handle. Better kitchen retailers often offer a "test drive" for thirty days with a full return policy. Keep trying styles until you find the tool that works best for your personal cooking and food preparation style.

Basic Knife Skills

Culinary terms often pop up in recipes that might be unfamiliar. Here are a few to familiarize yourself with:

- **Julienne:** To cut a food item into long, thin sticks of several inches in size and approximately 1/3-inch in diameter. Also called matchstick cut.

Julienne cuts of carrot.

- **Chop**: To coarsely cut food item in uneven chunks of approximately 1/2-inch in size. *(see example on following page)*
- **Dice:** To cut food item into evenly sized bits of approximately 1/4-inch in size. Can be accomplished by first cutting the food item into julienne, turning pieces at a right angle, then cutting into dice. *(see example on following page)*
- **Mince:** To cut food item into miniscule bits of less than 1/8-inch in size by repeatedly wielding the blade against the food on a cutting board in increasingly small increments. Commonly used with garlic or onion, or aromatics like fresh herbs.
- **Ribbon**: To use a vegetable peeler lengthwise on a food item to create flowing curls. *(see example on following page)*
- **Sliver**: To cut food item into long, thin strips.
- **Disc**: To cut food item across the width into circular shapes, as in a carrot or zucchini squash.
- **Flower**: To cut food item such as carrot or zucchini into discs, then selectively carve to resemble a flower. Or, to cut small portions off a cruciferous vegetable's stalk. Bite-sized broccoli and cauliflower pieces are often called flowerettes.

Less is More

Portion control is critical to outstanding food presentation and enjoyment. When a plate is too crowded, the diner often fails to appreciate the care with which food has been prepared. Even simple foods like Mom's famous Sunday afternoon spaghetti should be presented beautifully and cleanly, with a touch of fresh herbs or greenery for garnish.

In the second photo, the smaller portion size will encourage diners to savor the complexity of flavors – and stay awake through dessert!

Way too many carbs for any one waistline!

Create more white space on the plate to ensure the perfect portion size.

When serving a tasting portion or first course, use cocktail or bread plates. Here, a wine-glazed sea scallop sits atop an herb-infused nest of spaghetti squash.

Long, delicate curls of vegetables are a brilliant garnish for meats and salads. Ribbons can be sautéed in a bit of olive oil and sea salt and served in place of pasta – healthy *and* beautiful!

From front to back, carrots cut into dice, chop, and disc.

TIP

Gather vintage wooden cutting boards to use as the foundation for your buffet presentations.

Cutting Boards

The tried and true wooden cutting board of Grandma's day is not always your best option when it comes to sanitation. Items like poultry, fish, and meat can quickly contaminate the wood fibers if not properly cleaned. The better option is a set of colored flexible cutting sheets. Each is labeled and color-coded for use with a specific type of food so confusion and cross-contamination are all but eliminated.

For eco-friendly options, consider boards made of renewable resources like bamboo and acacia.

Food Presentation Tools

If you're ready to take your kitchen to the next level, consider these must-have tools to make it easier to present food beautifully.

Apple
slicer
Potato
slicer
Chefmate

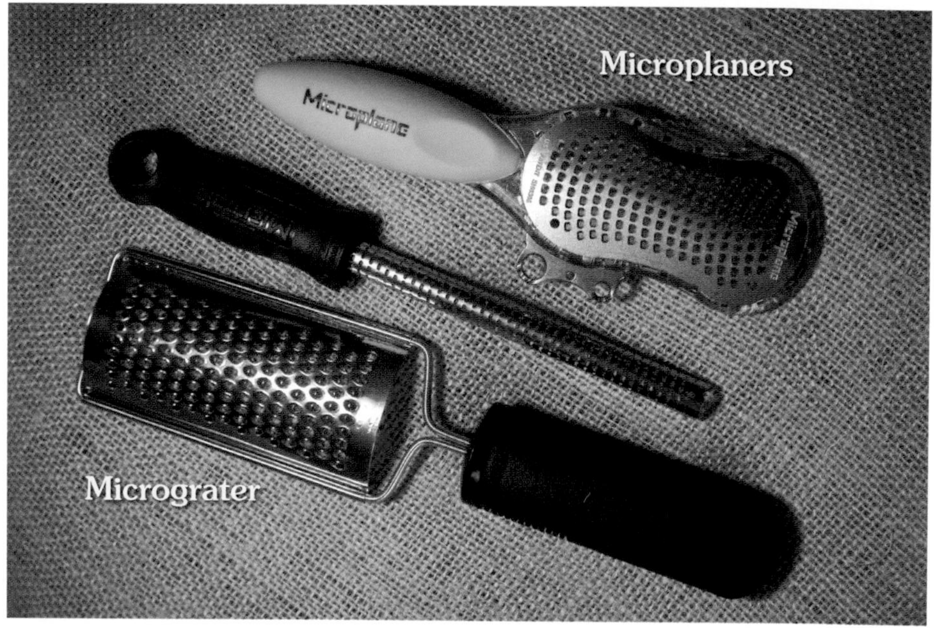
Microplaners
Microplane
Micrograter

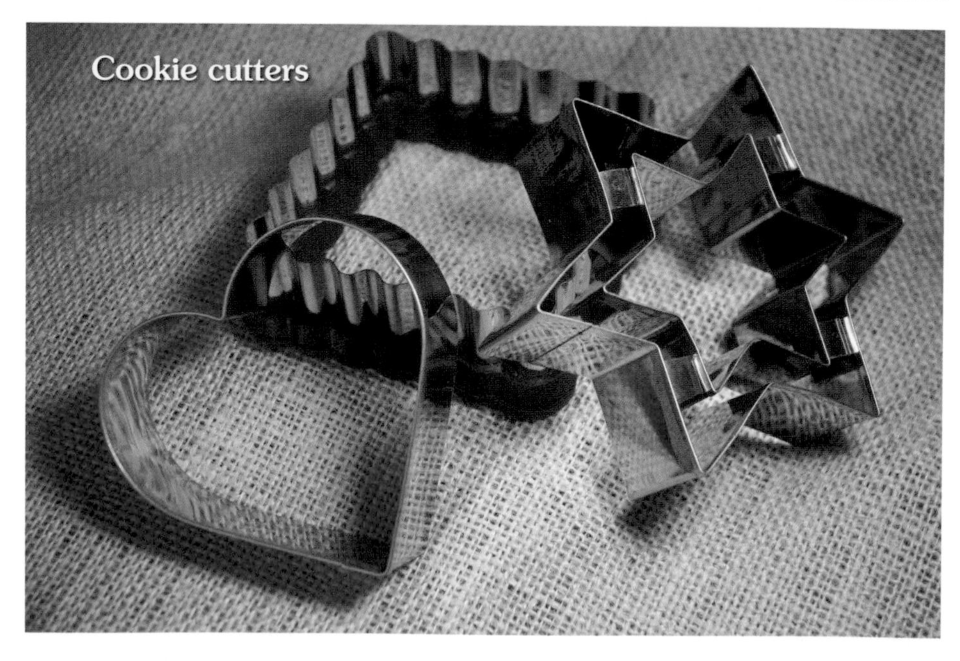
Cookie cutters

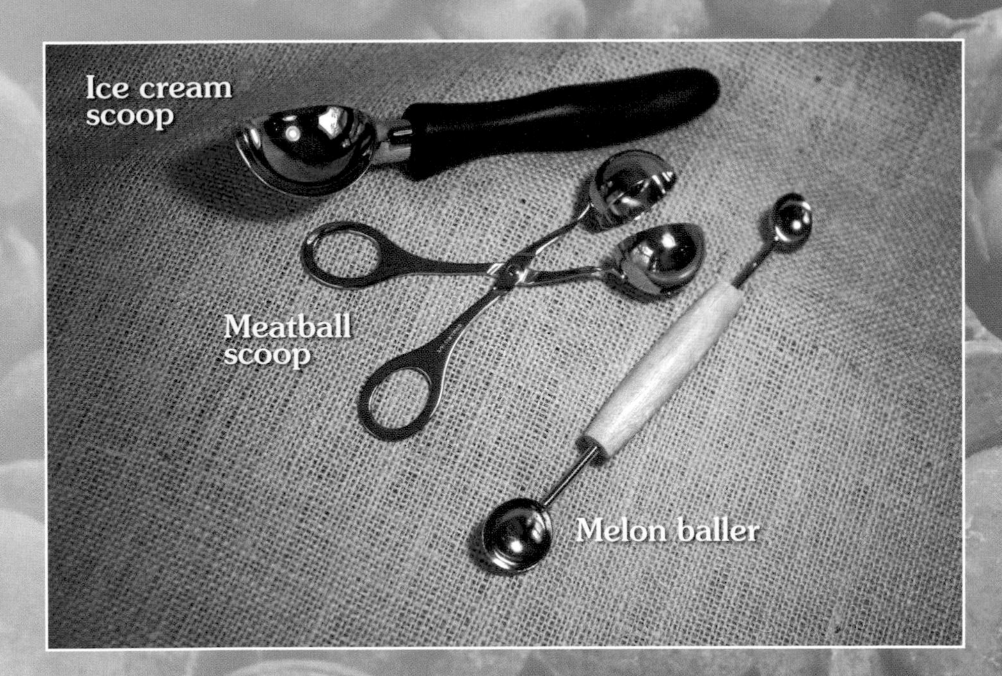
Ice cream scoop
Meatball scoop
Melon baller

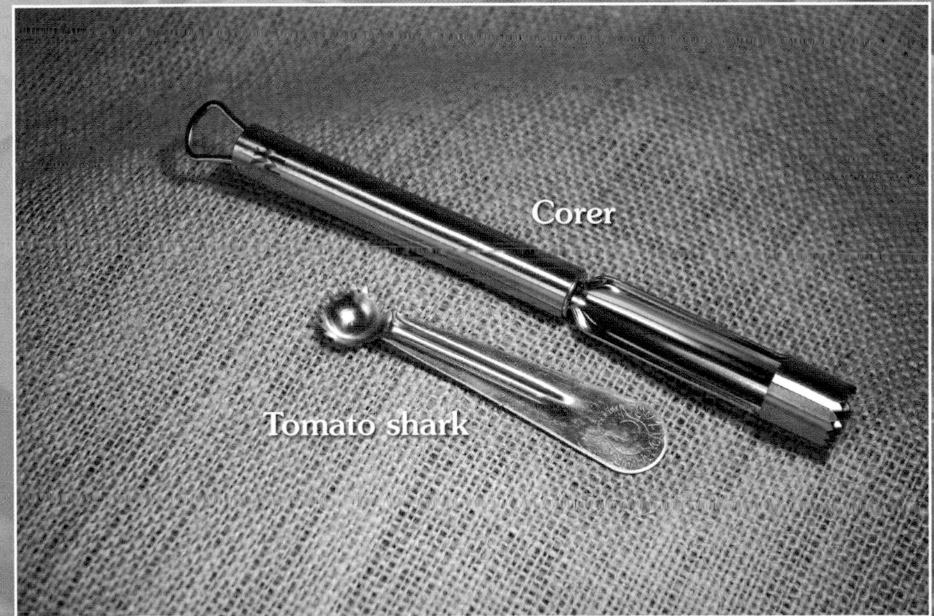
Corer
Tomato shark

Butter curler
Chocolate shaver

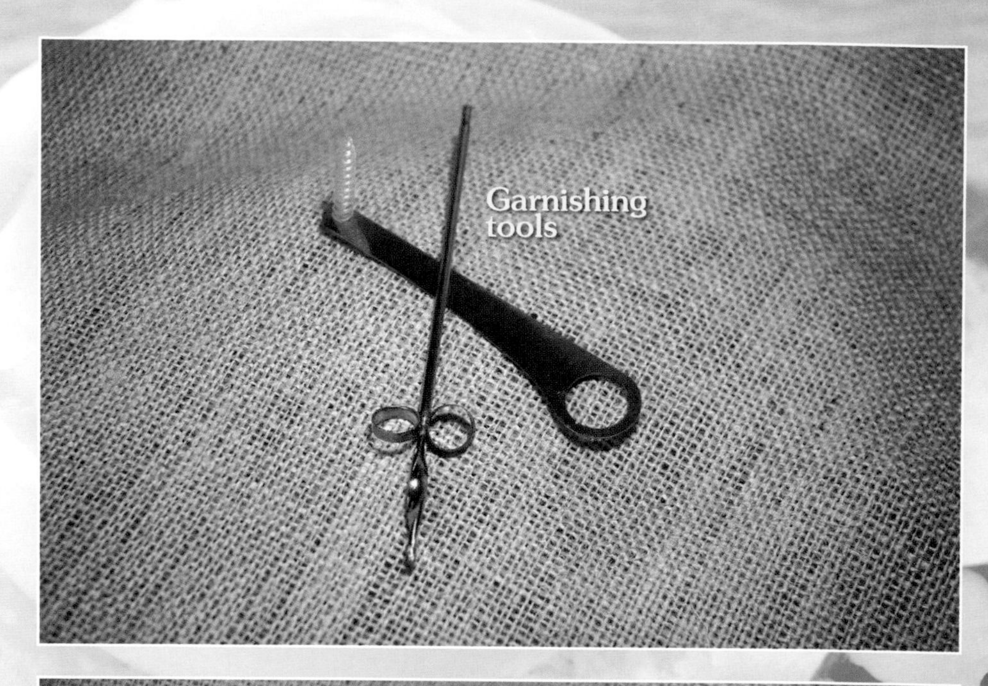
Garnishing
tools

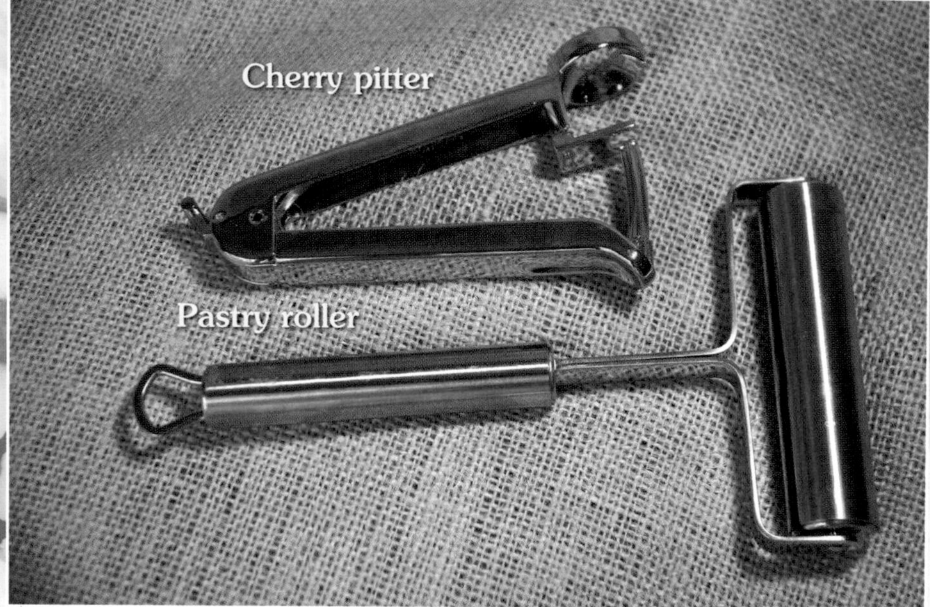
Cherry pitter
Pastry roller

Ginger
grater
Pastry
tamper
Butter pats

"An egg is always an adventure; the next one may be different."

— Oscar Wilde

The Perfect Hard-Cooked Egg

The art of cooking hard-boiled eggs is in the timing. Here, clockwise from bottom left, eggs have been immersed in slowly boiling water for four, five, six, seven, eight, and nine minutes, then plunged into an ice water bath to cool.

If you make egg salad with a combination of nine-minute eggs and one or two five-minute eggs, the salad color will be a lovely yellow.

Helpful hint: Lower eggs one at a time into boiling water using a slotted spoon to avoid cracking.

Timing is everything when it comes to eggs.

Broccoli slaw takes on new dimension when shaped by a 3-inch ring and centered on a pretty plate. Simply position the ring over the serving platter, fill with desired ingredients, and lift gently. Compressing the food slightly will help to retain the round shape once the ring is removed.

A melon baller is the perfect implement to make bite-sized scoops of chocolate hazelnut ice cream. Arrange the serving dish with a few chocolate dipped strawberries, two puddles of chocolate ganache, a sprinkling of toasted hazlenuts, and the ice cream.

Surprise and delight breakfast guests with cheerful daisy-shaped eggs.

Bakers rely on wire cake levelers to ensure smooth, uniform layers on their finished cakes. Simply allow cake to cool slightly, adjust the leveler to the appropriate height, and skim across the surface.

Far left:
Pastry chefs often rely on sections of pre-cut PVC pipe when creating elegantly shaped desserts. Your local hardware store will stock these dishwasher-safe tools in varying sizes. The tricks are simple. Line a baking sheet with parchment paper. Cut a sheet of acetate (old-fashioned office transparencies work well) to fit the circumference of the PVC. Set the acetate inside and it will settle against the shape of the curved container. Fill with mousse and refrigerate.

Left:
To unmold, use a metal spatula to lift the chilled dessert in its pipe onto the serving plate. Slip the pipe section off, carefully unwrap the acetate from the mousse and dress to serve.

Use cookie cutters to cut intricate shapes from fudgy brownies. Arrange on a serving plate then use a plastic stencil to apply just a tiny bit of frosting. The effect is fancy, but the technique is extremely simple to do. Instant dessert drama!

Lightweight plastic stencils are inexpensive and easy to clean. To use, center stencil on food or plate to be decorated. Using a flexible spreader, fill stencil with thick sauce, frosting, or confectioner's sugar. Starting from one corner, lift stencil gently to reveal design. For a special party, consider creating initial monograms on presentation plates for each guest.

Vintage button-topped skewers of roasted grapes adorn a sparkling wine cocktail.

Parchment is one of the most versatile wraps in the kitchen. It provides a non-stick disposable base for baking that won't add extra fat to the foods you prepare. Sandwiches wrapped in parchment are not only pretty, but also practical – the parchment won't stick to foods, but holds in crumbs from fresh-baked breads.

Flexible silicone molds come in hundreds of shapes. Here, a summery fruit drink is frozen to make flower-shaped ice cubes. The benefit? Drinks won't get watered down. Try this technique with coffee cubes in a cold glass of cinnamon milk for a delicious iced beverage. And who says wine glasses should be reserved just for wine? Enjoy a non-alcoholic drink with the same grandeur as a glass of one of your favorite vintages – add a little ceremony to your weeknight!

The butane torch is the preferred tool for caramelizing the sugar crust on *crème brulee*. It can also be used to create a variety of other foods like parmesan *tuiles*. Individual serving dishes of creamy mac and cheese get a crunchy crust with the help of a tablespoon of freshly grated sharp cheddar and a butane torch.

Pie Crust and Pastry

Every kitchen should be stocked with two highly versatile ingredients: refrigerated ready-made pie crust and frozen puff pastry sheets. These two staples can be transformed into any number of culinary delights at a moment's notice, from hors d'oeuvres to luscious entrees, to sinful desserts. Though homemade might be the sentimental favorite, these are two convenience foods worth stocking at all times.

Frozen sheets of puff pastry are extremely versatile. Tear off irregular shaped pieces and shape into free-form tart shells. Fill with seasoned pan-roasted vegetables, sprinkle with extra virgin olive oil, and bake until crust is golden and puffy. The vegetables will continue to cook, and the finished dish will taste like a slow-baked ratatouille – in a quarter of the time.

Fruit pies look especially beautiful with a lattice top crust. Dough may be cut with a crimped pastry cutter, or cut into long strips and gently rolled with fingertips before arranging. To assemble the lattice crust, align horizontal crust strips across the pie at intervals of about 1 1/2-inches. Place the first vertical strip and weave over and under the horizontal strips until the opposite side of the crust is reached. Repeat, alternating pattern of over and under from the crust edge. When all strips have been laid out, fold excess dough into pie crust edge and seal with a decorative thumb-forefinger pinch. Brush dough with beaten egg for a golden finish. When ready to cook, cover crust edges loosely with foil and remove halfway through baking.

TIP

When candles have lost their power to light, give them new purpose as buffet risers. These birch bark pillars add texture and dimension to the rustic tabletop.

Plates and Presentation

To present food beautifully, cooks are licensed to be creative. Instead of using paints and markers, the artistic tools of the cook's trade are fruit and vegetable purees, gravy and sauce reductions, and flavored creams in squeeze bottles and pastry bags. Cooked meats and pastas become canvases for creative interpretation. And the existing pattern on a plate can inspire creative interpretation.

An understanding of the basic principles of graphic design will help you to evaluate the dinner plate and food presentation with a fresh eye. Here's what you need to know:

- **White space**: Leaving enough empty space on a plate to make the items arranged become the primary focus.
- **Balance**: When items to the left and right of the center point are equally weighted in terms of visual perception.
- **Texture**: Including items of varying surface texture to create a stimulating visual display.
- **Dimension**: Arranging items in layers and with height to create a three-dimensional display that can be enjoyed from many vantage points.

Another key element in the success of your food presentation is understanding how to use pattern. Patterned plates with an overall design look best with solid color foods and a weighted center. Plates with rim designs will act as a frame for the food being presented.

Let's take a look at how pattern influences presentation.

Don't overcrowd serving plates. The square shape of this sweet violet platter is repeated in the individual ganache-coated brownies and the arrangement on the plate.

In this antique Chinese bowl, a bed of steamed green beans supports spicy noodles. The rose arrangement of the tender pork strips adds a finishing touch to this one-dish meal.

Presenting Food on Patterned Plates

Antique dinner plates are often the size of today's luncheon plates. As our nation has grown in girth, so has the size our dinner plates. The serving space on a typical dinner plate has increased in size from about eight or nine inches in diameter 50 years ago to nearly 12 inches now. Some restaurant presentation plates top 14 inches, which are great for a singular, spectacular presentation, but not so terrific for everyday use. The increase in physical serving space on dinner plates has led to larger portion sizes, a higher percentage of fat and calories, and an ever-expanding waistline for many diners.

So think of this added benefit of using Grandma's best Haviland: built-in portion control.

When china patterns feature intricate decorative details, focus food presentation on the center of the plate. Here, a duo of chevre fritters is flanked by a circle of thyme jelly. The arrangement harmonizes with the plate design, and the topping of sprigs of lemon thyme and German thyme mirrors the fine lines in the pattern.

TIP

Don't worry if your place settings don't match. Using multiple patterns of dinnerware can create a colorful and elegant table.

When building a meal's theme around heirloom china, take your color cues from the pattern, and design your menu with foods in hues that complement.

"Context and memory play powerful roles in all the truly great meals in one's life."
— Anthony Bourdain

The plate design of milk chocolate and raspberry swirls is echoed in the colors of this dense fudge cake and berries. To maintain an artful composition, plate dessert to one side and add elements sparingly to complement the pattern.

Patterned plates look best with solid color food presentations, like this butternut squash soup garnished with edible organic flowers.

Unusual shapes make for an interesting presentation. This octagonal Asian-inspired plate is an excellent choice for a sampling of steamed dumplings with a generous drizzle of soy-seasoned sauce.

Always be sure to check bowls and platters for safe food use. If the dish bottom bears a message about it being used for décor only, or if you are uncertain about suitability, move on to another plating option, or layer plates. High lead content in some decorative ceramics can make them unsafe for food use. You might also investigate melamine platters with intricate patterns. Here sesame noodles look stunning – even on a hard plastic platter.

When serving a clear soup like this beautiful borscht, consider the simplicity of glass bowls to highlight the ingredients. In this case, the richness of jewel-toned beets takes center stage.

When displaying elegant, beautiful finger food, opt for a simple serving platter such as this two-tiered metal platter.

Honor heirloom china with an extra special presentation at meal time. Here, lobster claws stand ready to mingle with creamy sherry crab and lobster bisque during a tableside pour.

Consider Shape and Size

More and more, dinnerware designers are creating plates with unusual shapes and sizes to add an artistic element to dinner service. Glassware artisans push the design limits and create striking pieces worthy of permanent display. Baking pans, too, are now available in almost any shape and size, from doll figurines to racing cars to six-tier castle creations.

Before you decide which direction to take on the technical components of a dinner service, consider all shapes and sizes of dinnerware available to you. Take a chance on something out of the ordinary to add a sense of drama to your food presentation.

Coffee on a foggy morning becomes a ritual to savor when served with delicate vintage china and lace.

Showcase delicate foods on contrasting, solid plates. Filled cucumber cups stand out against the deep blue of this serving plate.

Choose glassware that complements the tone of the cocktail within. Here, the gentle curves of these brilliant turquoise stems flare out to a wide brim – perfect for refreshing key lime drinks. Don't worry about matching all of your glasses. If you find a lovely pair in a color that you love, begin a collection and be on the lookout for unique pieces.

High-end dishware manufacturers experiment with plating shapes. Here, a four-compartment plate is perfect for a tapas-style sampler of roasted tomatoes, roasted peppers, black olives, and prosciutto. Top with a sprig of fresh basil and your presentation is at once elegant and appetizing.

The basic nut bowl gets a lift with this unusual serving piece. This would also be an excellent platter for salad or ice cream toppings.

Succulent summer blackberries and blueberries highlight the curved shape of the Bundt butter cake with sweet glaze. Search for specialty cake pans in the baking section of your local cookware shop. Remember, these pans have multiple uses besides cakes – fill with water, berries, and mint leaves and freeze for a statement ice ring, shape luncheon salads for buffet presentations and bake a generous portion of family-style meatloaf.

"I consider the discovery of a dish which sustains our appetite and prolongs our pleasures as a far more interesting event than the discovery of a star."
—Henrion de Pensey

The s'more grows up when a butane torch is used to coax marshmallows into delicious submission. Nestled between fluted cinnamon pastry cookies dusted in graham cracker crumbs, this dessert is made all the more decadent by its puddle of chocolate ganache on a small white plate.

Unusual shapes in serving ware command attention. Here, classic white is refined by sleek curves that highlight the simplicity of a roast beef and sautéed mushroom sandwich. The individual server of *au jus* gravy is just right for dipping.

Add variety to your meals with individual portions of composed butters like chipotle lime, sun dried tomato, and lemon tarragon. Dinner guests will be able to choose the flavor that suits their tastes.

Mini sauce containers are perfect for tableside service of dinner gravies, pan sauces, and salad dressings. The secret to perfect breakfast presentation is to provide guests with individual boats of syrups. Sweetened Swedish lingonberries become a plate feature while allowing sugar-dusted panettone French toast to remain deliciously crispy. If lingonberries aren't readily available, substitute whole berry cranberry sauce.

Sauçing Confidence

> *"Sauce: The one infallible sign of civilizations and enlightenment. A people with no sauces has one thousand vices; a people with one sauce has only nine hundred ninety-nine. For every sauce invented and accepted, a vice is renounced and forgiven."*
>
> *—Ambrose Bierce*

Fancy restaurants around the world know how to impress patrons with exquisite foods presented artistically. Much of that on-plate drama comes from basic saucing methods. We'll call these methods the puddle, the drizzle, the streak, and the paint.

- **The Puddle:** Sauce is pooled across the bottom of the plate and food item is placed at the center for presentation. Puddled sauce can be applied with a spoon or small ladle. Rimmed plates work best for this presentation.

This glistening ruby pear was simmered in spiced winter wine until tender. For more intense flavor, add a cinnamon stick while simmering. Puddle sauce on the plate and arrange cored pears for servcie. An alternate method of serving is vertical fan style. To prepare fruit for fan-style slice and eat presentation, hold poached pear by the stem and slice downward through the fruit's length while keeping the stem section intact. Gently fan cored, sliced pears in sauce and serve.

- **The Drizzle:** Sauce is applied sparingly in an irregular fashion around and over the food. This can be done with a spoon or plastic squirt bottle.
- **The Streak:** Sauce is applied with a spoon in several circles around food. The back of the spoon is then dragged quickly through sauce to create soft lines.
- **The Paint:** Food is arranged on plate. Sauce is applied with spoon or ladle to remaining white space, and "painted" to create a design.

The salad takes on new dimension when drizzled with aged balsamic reduction. Don't worry about perfection with this technique. A quick drizzle complements the flavor of these slow-roasted vegetables without overwhelming their delicate nature.

Think of your plate as a blank canvas. Fan meats in one direction, veggies in the other. Create abstract shapes with a delicate sauce to connect the two. Meats and vegetables will retain their individual flavors, and your sauce will become the focus of the meal.

Black sesame crusted tuna over sliced sweet peppers is adorned with a citrus wedge and an artistic streak of soy glaze.

"The preparation of good food is merely another expression of art, one of the joys of civilized living..."

—Dione Lucas

Arranging Meats

"In the hands of an able cook, fish can become an inexhaustible source of perpetual delight."
—Jean-Anthelme Brillat-Savarin

Succulent meats and fish often take center stage at the dinner table. But will your meal be family-style or will plates be presented one at a time? Do you want a help-yourself station set up counterside with drinks or do you want to wow your guests with a dynamic, personalized presentation that includes saucing each portion individually at the table?

Just like those high-drama saucing techniques, chefs rely on several basic meat presentation methods to define the perception of their meals. We'll call them The Fan, The Mound, The Roast, The Chop Stack, and The Drape.

- **The Fan:** Individual portion of meat is sliced in uniformly thin pieces, kept together at one end and fanned out at the other across the plate.
- **The Mound:** Meat is sliced and mounded high on a serving platter or cutting board.
- **The Roast:** Whole roast meats are positioned at the center of a serving platter, often surrounded by vegetables.
- **The Chop Stack***:* Individual chops are arranged with bones up, criss-cross fashion, to create a multi-dimensional display.
- **The Drape.** Vegetables or starches are used as a base for a singular piece of meat to be draped across. Meat is often topped by vegetables, herbs, or drizzled sauce.

TIP

Try cooking in parchment packets. Begin with a sheet of parchment paper three times the length of the widest part of your meat. At the paper's center add vegetables, seasonings, and a teaspoon of broth. Fold the parchment over the food as if you were folding a letter. Pinch packet ends together. Place packet on baking sheet and cook. Slide packet onto dinner plate and serve piping hot. Guests will enjoy the showmanship!

Crispy skin duck breast is the perfect choice to serve in a slim-slice fan on the serving plate. Accent with a fruit wine sauce and garnish of Italian parsley to make an elegant, classic presentation. The Bing cherries were prepared using the cherry pitting tool, then halved with a paring knife.

Marinated flank steak and other meats tempt diners when sliced thinly and mounded on the cutting board for immediate enjoyment. This is a terrific buffet presentation. Preserve the juices of extra steaks by slicing meat just before serving.

A succulent pork roast is framed by steamed miniature vegetables, pan roasted tomatoes and sweet peppers, and grilled zucchini rolls. For maximum visual impact and to enable tableside carving, present the roast whole and garnish with a few sprigs of fresh herbs.

A barbecued and sliced chicken breast balances roasted vegetables on the plate. To maintain proper portion control, rice is served "timbale" style and topped with fresh rosemary. To create, compress hot rice into a small bowl and invert onto serving plate.

A pair of succulent lamb chops sits atop a rosemary sprig and shares plate space with butter-browned pattypan squash.

Pan-roasted tilapia with diced pepper hash and fresh thyme looks elegant atop a block of neatly arranged asparagus tips.

"The fact is that it takes more than ingredients and technique to cook a good meal. A good cook puts something of himself into the preparation – he cooks with enjoyment, anticipation, spontaneity, and he is willing to experiment."

—Pearl Bailey

Decorative Presentation Techniques

Present Food with Style

Simplicity in both cooking and streamlined presentation makes for a memorable meal. Though eye-catching, many presentation techniques are actually designed to add a note of functionality to food service. If a food is easy to eat **and** it's pretty, diners tend to enjoy their meals that much more.

So how can you elevate the ordinary breakfast into something worthy of recanting to friends? How can you dress up the mid-week dinner plate with pizzazz and taste? How can you honor a special occasion dessert and get an "I can't believe how good it looks" response from guests?

Use these simple techniques to take your food presentation skills to an artistic level.

Nothing is more delightful on a summer evening than a plate of grana padano ravioli drizzled in browned butter and topped with fresh picked sage. To add interest to your dinner table, investigate all types of colorful ready-made pasta available dried or fresh. When serving, use herbs and vegetables in contrasting colors for the most visual impact.

"Eating is not merely a material pleasure. Eating well gives a spectacular joy to life and contributes immensely to goodwill and happy companionship. It is of great importance to the morale."

—Elsa Schiaparelli

The fastest way to dress up a dinner plate is to experiment with unusual starches. Many people think of rice as a staple, but more often than not it becomes an afterthought. Study the varieties available to add color and interesting flavors to your table. From left to right, Thai red rice, China black rice, bamboo rice, forbidden rice, wild field rice blend. To add a punch of rich golden yellow to your dining palette, use saffron rice.

"Rice is a beautiful food. It is beautiful when it grows, precision rows of sparkling green stalks shooting up to reach the hot summer sun. It is beautiful when harvested, autumn gold sheaves piled on diked, patchwork paddies. It is beautiful when, once threshed, it enters granary bins like a (flood) of tiny seed-pearls. It is beautiful when cooked by a practiced hand, pure white and sweetly fragrant."

—Shizuo Tsuji

Take breakfast outside with these layered parfaits assembled in vintage crystal. Begin with a base layer of soft-crunchy granola, add a few tablespoons of yogurt working from the center outward, top with fresh or juicy canned fruit, then repeat the process. Use yogurt sparingly to preserve the distinction of individual layers.

Use coffee mugs to serve kid-friendly breakfast burritos with applewood bacon and smoked ham. Mixing the eggs directly in the pan will result in yellow and white bits in the finished product. For a more uniform pale yellow color, whisk eggs in a separate bowl, then add to cooking pan. Helpful hint: to prevent filling from spilling out of the burrito, fold over the bottom edge after filling then roll.

A perfectly sliced piece of herb quiche is adorned by a rustic topping of slow-roasted tomatoes.

Caviar feels like an indulgent treat. Unless you're able to spring for the more luxurious Beluga or Osetra, you might satisfy your caviar craving with the Romanoff red and black you can find in the canned fish section of your local grocery. These are inexpensive, make a big impact, and add some drama to your party appetizer selection. Dip plain breadsticks in whipped cream cheese then roll ends in caviar. Arrange spoke wheel fashion and serve immediately to retain the crunchiness of the breadsticks.

Bread bowls offer a two-for-one treat when filled with luscious bacon-topped seafood chowder. Rings of mini sweet peppers add a punch of color to this beachside snack. A multi-leveled display like this is the perfect use for wooden cutting boards and chopping blocks.

"One of the very nicest things about life is the way we must regularly stop whatever it is we are doing and devote our attention to eating."

—Luciano Pavarotti

Birthdays will be extra special when a layer cake is dressed up with pirouette cookies and a bold ribbon.

TIP

Bake cakes a day or two ahead of an event. Prepare as directed, allowing to cool before wrapping individual layers in cling wrap to store in a cool, dry place. Frost, fill, and decorate layers the morning of serving and chill. For maximum flavor, allow cakes to rest at room temperature for at least an hour before slicing.

Present beautifully swirled cupcakes on a bed of jelly beans. The cupcakes will stay in place – and guests will enjoy the second sweet treat!

For a fabulous one-minute dessert with ready-made ingredients, take one slice of store-bought pound cake and slice it into two thin sections. Layer whipped cream and two to three sliced strawberries. Top with a sprig of fresh mint and enjoy!

"Of soup and love, the first is best."
—Spanish Proverb

Top off a bowl of Tuscan bean soup with prosciutto wrapped breadsticks for crunch and flavor.

Lunch service need not be overly fussy. A grilled sandwich is cut on the diagonal and stacked. Take it outside, pour a cold glass of beer, and enjoy your outdoor dining spaces.

Honor tradition by serving mini versions of the classic Coke® float. Fill glass with vanilla bean ice cream, top with Coke®, and finish off with a maraschino cherry. These mini fountain glasses are the perfect snack size for an indulgent treat – just enough to satisfy a craving for old-fashioned fun.

TIP

Fresh summer strawberries need no adornment other than a beautiful bowl, a healthy dose of sunshine, and a sprinkling of sugar.

A single ripe strawberry is the only garnish you'll need for a muddled key lime and strawberry smash. Simply dip strawberry in sugar, spear with a short skewer and rest on the glass rim for guests to enjoy.

The classic rainy day combo of grilled cheese and tomato soup gets a lift from a handmade lavender platter and a fun square soup bowl. Arrange the sandwiches geometrically.

A late night snack of ham and gruyere and reuben mini paninis is served in a parchment-lined basket over a bed of toasted cheese puffs. Skewers help keep sandwiches fresh-from-the-grill crispy.

Hand-painted plates were popular in Victorian times and at the turn of the 20th Century, but they rarely came in sets. Dust off precious family heirlooms to serve individual pecan Bundt cakes. The only adornment this dessert needs is a fine dusting of confectioner's sugar.

For added drama when presenting a singular item, choose a bold serving platter that complements the food's color. Arranging in stacks lends a bit of architectural interest to the plate.

Truffles and chocolate-covered fruit are an excellent choice to serve with chilled champagne. Instead of setting up in the kitchen or dining room, consider other beautiful locations in your home. Here, a table rests in perfect range for an impromptu concert.

"I live on good food, not fine words."
—Jean-Baptiste Molière

The simplicity of slivered sweet peppers in Asian chili oil dressing can't be beat. Pair the zesty flavors with a geometric bowl and a pair of chopsticks. If you prefer a slaw-like salad, use your chef's knife to cut peppers lengthwise into strips then repeat the process until you've achieved the width of pepper strips you desire.

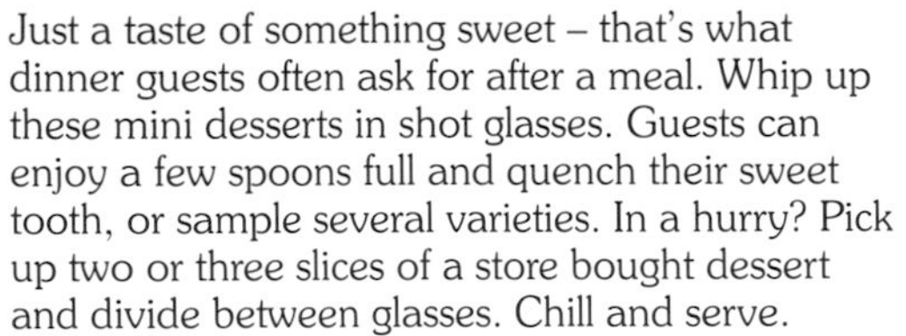

Just a taste of something sweet – that's what dinner guests often ask for after a meal. Whip up these mini desserts in shot glasses. Guests can enjoy a few spoons full and quench their sweet tooth, or sample several varieties. In a hurry? Pick up two or three slices of a store bought dessert and divide between glasses. Chill and serve.

For a refreshing seasonal alternative to plain chilled water, add thinly sliced cucumbers, a twist of lemon, and a sprig of fresh rosemary to the glass.

"Only when a chef changed the way you saw the world, through cooking, did food truly become art, and that was rare indeed."

—Michael Ruhlman

Carved Cantaloupe

Using a serrated and pointed-end food decorator, carve a scalloped edge into a section of cantaloupe and fill with balled fruits and berries. Drizzle with tupelo honey for a sweet final note.

Beautify your morning routine by using egg cups to present soft-boiled eggs. Shaping the toasts adds an extra special touch to this simple presentation.

You could just toss these fillo dough tyropita on a plate to serve, but isn't it so much more fun to take advantage of their natural shape and turn them into a pinwheel reminiscent of carefree summer days?

Add a mozzarella snowman with calamata olive eyes, buttons, and hat to your holiday antipasti platter. For stability, use a six-inch skewer through the snowman's center and position in a small white bowl. Top with a carrot peel scarf. To build the surrounding snowbank, dress plate with greens, then top with varying sizes of fresh mozzarella slices. If it's to your taste, add a dusting of sea salt over the cheese to simulate snowflakes.

Sometimes, fresh-from-the-oven crisps are best presented right on the cooling rack for guests to enjoy.

A newspaper, a pretty napkin, and a morning mug of granola in fresh milk is all you need to start the day off right.

For a quick, fresh dessert in the summertime, arrange blueberries in a triangle on a petite serving dish. Continue stacking blueberries in progressively smaller triangles until you top the pyramid with a single berry. Coat the berries in a glaze of orange blossom honey, sprinkle with orange peel, and top with a twist of rind. Enjoy!

Bruschetta is a wonderful appetizer, but it can also be an extraordinary light dinner with a chilled glass of wine. Rub thin slices of day-old Italian bread with a clove of garlic then grill in a bit of olive oil. When nice and crunchy, remove from heat to cool on a wire rack. Toasts can be made ahead and stored in an airtight bag for twenty-four hours. When ready to serve, spread with marinated tomatoes, slivers of grilled meats, fresh chopped herbs, and bits of buffalo mozzarella. For a hot/cool combo, use your butane torch to lightly melt the cheese while keeping the veggie layer refreshingly cool.

Asparagus should be served vivid green and tender-crisp – not yellowish and wilted. To achieve the perfect asparagus, heat a pot of water to a rolling boil. Drop cleaned asparagus into water and cook until it turns bright green. This should only take a few minutes. Immediately plunge the stalks into a bowl of ice water to stop the cooking process. Sprinkle with fleur de sel and serve as a finger food appetizer with lemon aioli. If a few tips break off, don't worry. Simply arrange them into a decorative pattern on top of the whole stalks – they'll still be delicious.

Use a gently warmed ice cream scoop to make perfect balls of your favorite treat. Dip in warm water between scoops to maintain the round shape. Some ice cream scoops are fluid filled and meant to be warmed in the microwave for 30 seconds. The added heat makes scooping a cinch!

Tacos are one of those hard-to-serve foods that often make pretty presentation difficult. For a creative solution, use clean polished river rocks to lend support to these handheld snacks. To solidify the presentation, consider using flat-bottomed crispy taco shells.

"A significant part of the pleasure of eating is in one's accurate consciousness of the lives and the world from which the food comes."

—Wendell Berry

The traditional holiday cheese ball takes new shape with the addition of roasted almonds. Press nuts into oval shaped ball of cheese in neat overlapping rows. Add a sprig of fresh pine for a note of authenticity.

Leftover flank steak becomes a delectable bite-sized treat when stuffed with slow-roasted tomatoes and herbed goat cheese.

Condiments need not be displayed in dull containers. Consider visiting the crystal cabinet for wide-mouth glasses that can easily be accessed by guests. Vary heights for more visual interest.

Lagniappe

The Cajun term for something extra. Always remember to add lagniappe to your everyday meals by presenting food beautifully.

The All-American classic BLT gets a facelift – without bread. Here, a medium sized tomato is hollowed out using a bird's eye knife. The tomato is filled with butter lettuce, chopped tomato and a few slices of crispy bacon. Remaining tomato bits are mixed with mayonnaise and spicy globe basil for a healthy dollop on a large sweet basil leaf.

A simple salad looks elegant when fruits and savory bits are artfully arranged. Here, butter lettuce, cling peaches, bacon, crispy smoked ham, goat cheese, and balsamic glaze work together for a simple, yet beautiful, presentation.

This fanciful winged creature was carved out of thin slices of peeled jicama (sometimes called Mexican potato). Add a few sliced grape tomatoes for contrast and serve white balsamic dressing on the side. Jicama is simple to carve. Use the tip of a bird's eye knife and make shallow, curving cuts. You can't go wrong; if you're unsure of your artistic abilities, go freeform. Abstract expression is all about creativity – anything goes. Whatever you create, guests will be delighted by the unexpected presentation!

Get Fancy the Easy Way

Fool the eye. In painting, the technique is called ***trompe l'oeuil.*** In magic, it's ***legerdemain***, or sleight of hand. In food presentation, the technique is about creating an illusion, fooling the eye, enticing the diner to believe that what has been accomplished on a plate was far more difficult than it actually was.

Illusion is what will transform an ordinary slice of jicama into a winged creature, or a handful of olives and toasted seeds into a garden flower, or an ordinary baby red potato into a golden rose. Culinary tricks will give shape to soft salads or height to mousse.

To achieve the masterful presentations on the following pages, you'll want to experiment with the knives and garnishing tools introduced in the picture glossary at the beginning of the book. You'll also need to find your courage to stack foods and create geometric arrangements on a plate. If the designs fall over, start again and keep trying new shapes until you find one that best highlights the food you've prepared.

While takeout cartons are perfectly serviceable, enhance the dining experience by arranging sushi on individual small white dishes. The white "canvas" of each small dish offsets the sculptural quality of the colorful sushi.

Serve melon in a stack of neat slices to highlight the beauty of summer-fresh color. Just a few dots of aged balsamic reduction are all you need to accent the flavors of the fruit.

Cookie cutters can be used to shape luncheon salads. Position on the serving plate, fill with salad and compress slightly. Top with a garnish of the salad ingredients. Here, a delicate chicken salad is adorned with crisp apple slices and a toasted pecan. To prevent apple slices from browning too quickly, dip in orange juice.

Serve mini cocktail breads by arranging in neat spirals. Here, scrap pieces of granite add levels to the display.

Just for fun, serve up an after school sundae treat of brownie balls. Use a large melon baller to shape brownies into delectable one-bite balls then mix with bite-sized balls of ice cream. For a quick placemat with easy clean-up, use a sheet of colored tissue paper.

Individual fruit tarts are easy to assemble. Simply use the pastry tamper to pack a 4-inch removable bottom fluted tart pan with your favorite cookie crust, top with whipped cream or custard and finish with concentric circles of fruit slices or berries. Chill, remove from pan and enjoy!

For a quick, impressive salad, arrange refrigerated grapefruit sections in a pinwheel design. Fill spaces with mandarin orange segments and accent with slivers of red onion. No dressing required – the fruit is juicy enough on its own!

Eight minutes. That's how long it takes to assemble this fabulous appetizer from start to finish using store-bought ingredients and a small spring-form pan with removable bottom. Of course, the flavors can be punched up with farm-grown, slow-simmered tomatoes. But in case you're short on time, keep your pantry and fridge stocked for those drop-in guests you still want to impress. Have seasoned, diced tomatoes on hand at all times, and sun-dried tomato paste to boost flavor. To assemble this layered treat, use the pastry tamper to pack a layer of crushed butter crackers that have been mixed with 1 Tablespoon melted butter. Layer chopped prosciutto, roasted and seasoned tomatoes, whipped cream cheese, pitted and halved Kalamata olives, and la pluma toasted pepita seeds. Chill until firm, release from spring-form pan, and serve with crackers or olive oil grilled toasts.

"One must always welcome guests sincerely, with a certain effusion of the heart, for when they come to your table they must already be happy with you."

—Baron Brisse

Pair foods with the color theme of your place settings. Here, a sunny deck garden becomes the perfect spot for a midday treat of white chocolate mousse with blueberries.

Decorative French country plates complement crisp Indian linens and blue and white pottery.

Play off the pattern in your china by using fruit as "paint" to enhance the image. Here, dots of *coulis de cassis* enhance blooms in the pattern and are topped by juicy raspberries. Dessert can be light and refreshing while still making a huge visual impact for diners.

To make these lovely potato roses, begin with firm red or golden new potatoes or a combination of the two. Holding the potato firmly in one hand, carefully use the tip of your bird's eye knife (or a hobby knife) to begin to make V-shaped 1/2-inch cuts in the rose. Work from the outside in until you reach the center point. Don't strive for perfection or you'll get frustrated. Once roses have been shaped, boil to the desired tenderness.

New potatoes can be carved into delicate roses then oven or pan roasted face down in butter until the "petals" are bronzed.

"The art of dining well is no slight art, the pleasure no slight pleasure."

—Michel Eyquem de Montaigne

A delightful way to serve fresh strawberries is to present them fan-style. To prepare, grip each strawberry by the stem and make thin slices lengthwise, keeping the berry's overall shape intact. Then, spread the attached slices fan-style and arrange on a beautiful plate. If you have a good supply of mint on hand, replace the strawberry stems with clusters of fresh mint leaves to make the presentation completely delicious.

Garnish a serving plate during the holidays with a red pepper poinsettia. Simply seed a red pepper and cut with the sharp tip of a knife into leaves. If desired, carve texture lines in the leaves and top with capers. On a similar note, orange peppers can be carved into delightful jack-o-lanterns at Halloween, and yellow peppers can be carved into a bouquet of fun flowers in the spring. Use your imagination.

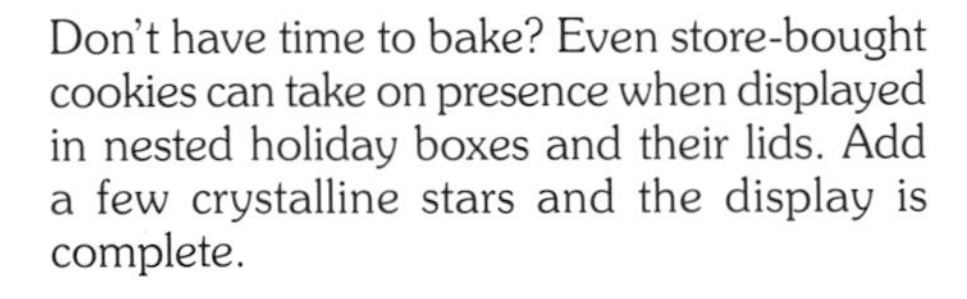

Don't have time to bake? Even store-bought cookies can take on presence when displayed in nested holiday boxes and their lids. Add a few crystalline stars and the display is complete.

Simple stacks of pickled beets and goat cheese make a striking first course or party appetizer. To prepare, make small balls of softened goat cheese and flatten between beet layers. Press slightly and garnish with fresh herbs. These can be sliced into wedges after chilling. An easy way to make a perfect stack is to compress beets and cheese in a shaping ring, then slide finished product through to serving platter.

"Good apple pies are a considerable part of our domestic happiness."

—Jane Austen

The apple blossom tart is a fresh take on mom's apple pie – it boasts all the delectable sweetness while being far less filling. Fit a five-inch removable bottom tart pan with your favorite crust. Arrange thin, curved slices of cinnamon sugar apples in concentric circles to emulate flower petals. Bake until golden and bubbly. To serve, simply remove the tart from the outer ring. This method takes a little longer to arrange than a basic apple pie, but the beautiful results are well worth the extra effort.

Be patriotic with summer berry tarts. Stars and stripes are easy to achieve with fresh blueberries, blackberries, raspberries, or strawberries. Simply layer a graham cracker crust with freshly whipped cream then arrange berries to enliven your holiday picnic table.

A birthday party reflects plenty of front-yard fun for little ones. Here, the "kid in a candy store" theme is displayed on a sectioned mirror (taken right from a wall!) topped with colorful candy and sweets. Don't be afraid to bring out grandma's beautiful crystal to enhance the appeal of the treats.

Working with Chocolate

For thousands of years, chocolate has been prized for its luxuriant quality. From its historical origin in Mexico, where the Olmec ground cocoa beans to brew into beverages, chocolate has developed into an international passion. In fact, annual United States chocolate sales are projected to surpass $18 billion. With a growing popularity, it makes perfect sense to incorporate chocolate products into your food presentations.

Plastic squeeze bottles are great tools for sauces, oils, icing, and chocolate. Heat chocolate disks in plastic bottle in microwave just until chocolate melts. Knead gently, cover tip with your thumb, and give bottle a hard shake down toward the tip to prevent air bubbles from ruining your design. On parchment-lined baking sheet, create shapes, initials, or words using consistent pressure. Chill until firm.

Carefully remove the chocolate work from parchment and position on dessert.

Varieties & Purpose

Before you can begin to work with chocolate, it is important to understand the varieties available and their purposes. This brief overview will help you make the proper selection when purchasing chocolate for use in cooking and eating.

- **Cocoa powder**: The resulting dry non-fat solid extracted from cocoa beans. Used in beverages, baking, and candy-making. Cocoa butter is the fatty extract of cocoa beans.
- **Ground chocolate:** Semi-sweet chocolate that has been pulverized.
- **Baking chocolate**: Semi-sweet, unsweetened, bittersweet, and white chocolate designated for baking. Often pre-portioned in one-ounce squares. If unsweetened, baking chocolate can also be called chocolate liquor. Sold in grocery stores.
- **Couverture chocolate**: Melted chocolate used for covering candies or baked goods. Contains a higher percentage of cocoa butter than other baking chocolates.
- **Eating chocolate:** Chocolate that is suitable for eating without any alteration.
- **White chocolate:** A combination of sugar, cocoa butter, and milk that solidifies and can be molded and melted like darker chocolate.

Key Recipe Terms

The next step in your chocolate education is understanding several key terms you might come across in your recipe search.

- **Bloom:** When cocoa butter or sugar comes to the surface of chocolate that has been warmed and cooled again. You might notice this if you purchase chocolate candies, enjoy a few, then refrigerate the remainder. Bloom does not harm the chocolate, but it will diminish the beauty of a presentation. See notes on chocolate storage below.
- **Tempering:** The process of heating, cooling, and reheating chocolate to specific temperatures to increase gloss in the finished product. Tempered chocolate is used in molds (like the infamous Easter bunnies) and to coat candies (like truffles).
- **Seizing:** When chocolate becomes grainy during melting. The oil content needs to be balanced. Add a teaspoon of vegetable oil and stir gently to incorporate.

TIP

Here's a helpful hint to avoid chocolate explosions in your kitchen: don't use water balloons as your base. They are too thin and won't withstand the warmth or weight of the chocolate.

To make beautiful chocolate cups, blow up a small latex balloon. Using a rolling motion, dip the balloon base in chocolate to coat. Allow to chill on baking sheet lined with parchment. When chocolate is firm, pop balloon and remove pieces.

The chocolate balloon bowl is perfect for filling to the brim with luscious deep dark ice cream and fresh sliced berries. Top it off with a bittersweet truffle and grab two spoons to share with a friend. To arrange chocolate cup at an angle, put a dollop of melted chocolate on the plate and affix cup.

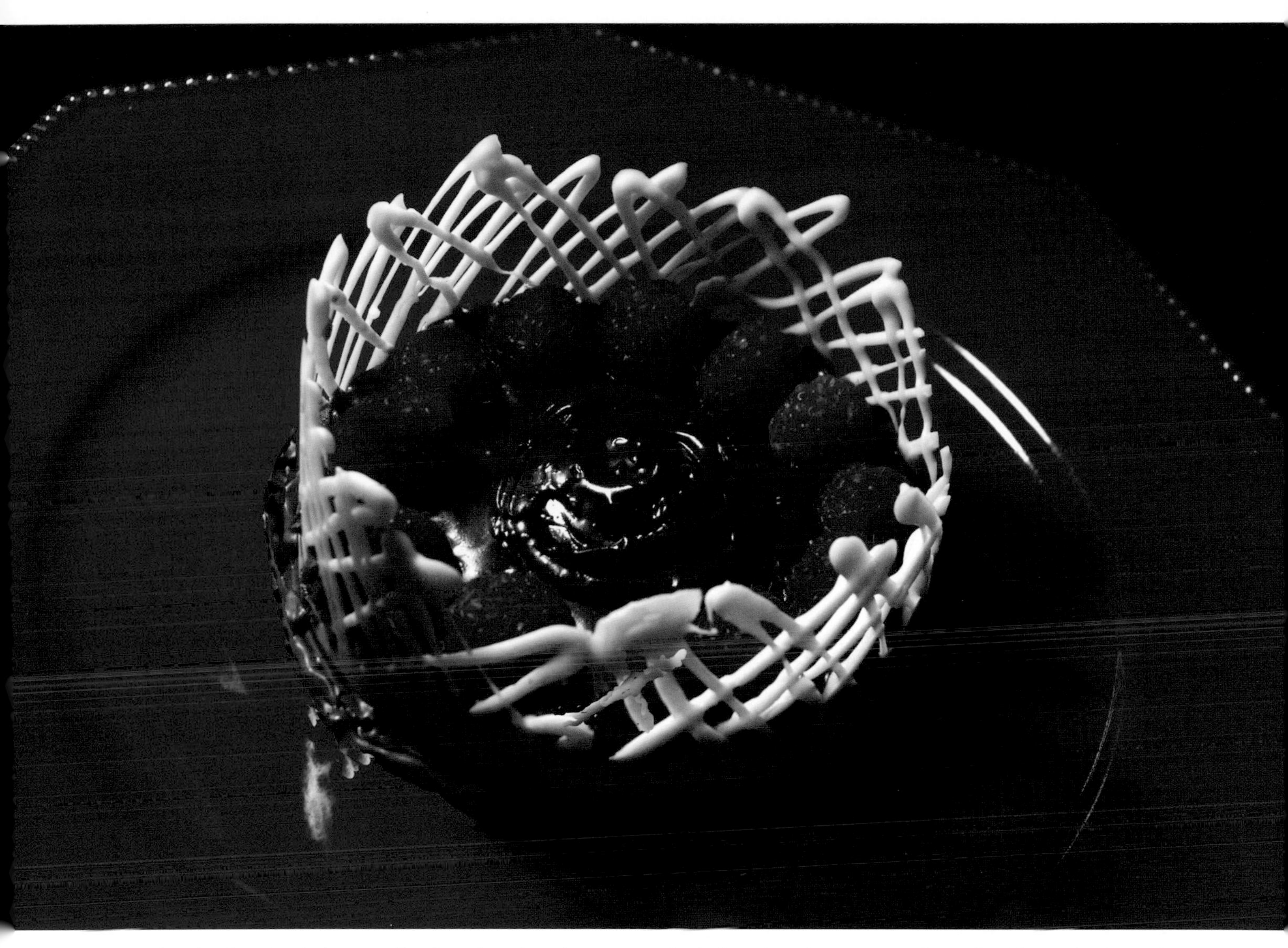

Drama goes hand in hand with desserts. For this white chocolate cage, melted white chocolate was piped onto flexible acrylic sheets then fitted against sides of removable bottom tart pan. Once chocolate has set, filling can be layered into the pan and topped as desired. This is a tricky procedure – take care not to let the sheets of chocolate collapse into the dessert center. To serve, remove the sides of the tart pan very carefully. Position on serving plate and gently peel away acrylic. Elegant and impressive!

"The only real stumbling block is fear of failure. In cooking you've got to have a what-the-hell attitude."
—Julia Child

Chocolate is a specialty item that comes in many tastes and textures. While chocolate chips are available in grocery stores, chocolate candy discs are available in the baking section of your local crafts store or online. The larger discs come in many colors and flavors, including vanilla, peanut butter, and mint. The discs are ideal for making lacy chocolate accents for desserts.

For a quick treat without the mess, dip marshmallows in melted chocolate and roll in sugar sprinkles. Pierce with a skewer to serve. Chocolaty goodness – no mess!

Great impact on a budget is simple with a luxurious display of store-bought chocolate treats – even crunchy cereals. Here, vintage pewter serveware is arranged on multiple levels. Simply unwrap candies, group in similar containers, and let your guests indulge in an easy to prepare dessert of bite-sized sweets.

Chocolate Storage

For maximum taste and enjoyment, chocolate should be stored in a cool, dry place. Ideally, temperature should be near 65 degrees Fahrenheit. If refrigeration or freezing is necessary due to high environmental humidity or heat, condensation on the chocolate can occur and may impact its ability to melt properly.

The simple luxury of chocolate dipped strawberries is unparalleled. The bonus for the entertainer is that they're simple to make. Choose strawberries with greenery attached, wash and pat dry with paper towels. Dipping chocolate is readily available at supermarkets in simple to use microwaveable containers. If you are unable to find dipping chocolate, melt over indirect heat one cup semi-sweet chocolate bits with one teaspoon solid vegetable shortening in a double boiler over simmering water.

"All you need is love. But a little chocolate now and then doesn't hurt."
—Charles M. Schulz

Chocolate can be your best friend in entertaining – it handles well, makes an impact, delivers on taste. To make these pointed accents, heat semi-sweet chocolate chips in a microwave safe bowl on medium high until melted. Spread chocolate on parchment-lined baking sheet. Refrigerate until firm. Using a chef's knife, cut triangles from the cold chocolate and use as a topper for mini-cups of whipped espresso mousse. Keep chilled until serving time.

Dress up a simple cup of cocoa with a dollop of fresh whipped cream and shaved Dutch chocolate.

Beautiful Buffets

Pleasing a crowd is always a balancing act of making sure you have enough food, making sure the variety is sufficient to keep guests interested and well-fed, and making sure the presentation is attractive enough to showcase your culinary talents and hard work. In addition, preparing for a buffet means juggling your schedule to compensate for multiple cooking times and temperature requirements.

The classic antipasto buffet is a feast for the senses. Aromas of the Mediterranean kitchen merge with the visual stimulation of myriad colors and textures. To keep guests nibbling, serve many varieties of cheese, cured meats, smoked fish, olives, breads, shellfish, and vegetables. Of course, a selection of olive oils and aged balsamic vinegar will allow guests to indulge according to personal taste. Arrange dishes on multiple levels to add dimension to your presentation. Since finger foods can be messy, be sure to include several stacks of extra napkins throughout your service space. Guests will appreciate the consideration. Here, tall thin breadsticks look elegant standing upright in a slim glass.

Petite fresh mozzarella perlini and grape tomatoes are threaded on slim stainless poultry lacers for an easy-to-indulge treat with a delicate touch.

Caterers and banquet managers rely on interior design principles to create dramatic tabletop displays. Here are a few to consider:

- **Create levels:** Levels on the tabletop add dimension and interest and allow for striking displays. These can be accomplished by using risers beneath the table linens, which are often made up of several matching cloths.
- **Ruche and bunch:** To disguise seams where cloths come together, ruche and bunch the fabric.
- **Use sparkle:** Always add a touch of glass to the display to catch the light.
- **Be wary of candles:** Candles on a buffet where guests will be reaching for foods are a fire hazard. If you intend to use candlelight, better to incorporate it on a side table or a mantel for effect. Better yet, use battery-operated flameless candles for complete safety.
- **Include a focal point:** In a long display, you might create focal points at both ends of the table, or draw the eye to the center with one grand, tall floral piece.
- **Keep dishes and implements to the side:** Make it simple for guests to pick up a plate then travel through the buffet.
- **Use spoon rests:** Nothing is more distracting than a cloth stained with sauces because no serving spoon rests were available.
- **Keep flammables away from heat sources:** If using liquid fuel, be certain to clear a wide swath around the lit canisters for safety.

Soak flat wooden skewers briefly in water to prevent from scorching while grilling shrimp.

TIP

If using citrus to marinate shellfish and other seafood, take care with respect to timing. The acids in citrus can "cook" these delicate proteins if allowed to marinate for too long. Consider adding juices just before cooking, or squeeze on foods afterwards as a flavor enhancer.

To make prosciutto roses, begin with a long strip of the meat. Roll the meat with the fat side on top, pinching bottom lightly to force the top to fan wider. When roll is complete, gently pull apart the "petals" at the top and arrange on serving platter.

Smoked capelin school on an oval dish next to prosciutto roses.

Layer fresh buffalo mozzarella with fresh basil, sliced tomatoes, and toasted pine nuts for a classic Caprese salad. Forget about perfection – this is all about savory taste. Drizzle with aged balsamic and extra virgin olive oil then top with cracked black pepper.

"In the Italian culture for hundreds of years, as long as Parmigiano Reggiano or prosciutto di Parma has been being made, it's been an expression of not only their hunger and of their love for things that taste good, but the artisanship of the products themselves."

— Chef Mario Batali

Clear a side table near the primary buffet to set up a serve-yourself wine bar. Feature several varieties of wine, along with a selection of red and white wine glasses. For a regional touch, offer a few wines from a local vineyard. Make sure to create levels using color-coordinated risers to add visual interest to your display.

"The dinner table is the center for the teaching and practicing not just of table manners but of conversation, consideration, tolerance, family feeling, and just about all the other accomplishments of polite society except the minuet."

— Miss Manners (Judith Martin)

Think outside the basket, literally. When presenting breads for a buffet, mix textures and shapes for the most interesting visual display. Farmers' markets often offer mix and match selections of fresh baked goods at reasonable prices.

Trays of individual crocks of zesty black bean chili give guests a head start on food selection. Portion out hot chili, keep warm in oven until serving time, and top with shredded cheese at the last minute for garnish. Roasted corn speckles the serving tray with texture.

An arrangement of mini gin cocktails awaits arriving party guests. Simply dip rim of shot glasses in water then in colored citrus sugar, fill with excellent quality gin and top off with a few slivers of lemon. Chill and serve. Preparing a few drinks in advance alleviates bartending duties at the beginning of a party.

Let guests get in on the fun and create their own desserts. Sugar cookies are ready to be frosted and decorated with an array of sprinkles and candies at a holiday party.

Get the brunch party started with stacks of bagel sandwiches layered with delicious ingredients.

Take breakfast outside with a simple brown bag buffet. Mini chalkboards point out the flavors of this Mitera Granola – Apple Pie, Almond Cherry, Georgia Peach, and Orange Roasted. Add a handful of spoons and pitcher of fresh milk and you're good to go!

The classic All-American seafood boil of seasoned lobsters, crawfish, corn, and potatoes gets an uplift from a scrolled ironwork bowl. If you're entertaining a large crowd, prepare several serving platters for intimate groups of guests to enjoy.

Be mindful of where you serve the foods you've taken time and effort to prepare. These tea sandwiches are as lovely as the garden setting they complement. Unifying the serving pieces lends a cohesive look to your table-scape. Consider using multiple small flower vases in a complementary color scheme to add dimension and texture to the tabletop.

Leftover boiled potatoes gain second life when pan-fried in olive oil with bacon crumbles and diced ham. To create, layer individual baking dishes with potato hash mixture, then top with a fresh egg and cracked black pepper. Bake in a moderate oven until egg is set. This is an excellent dish to serve at a help-yourself breakfast buffet.

White wine shimmers above a silver tray of sparkling ice. The "ice" is actually shaped acrylic bits that come in various shapes and can be found in the table décor or bridal décor sections of decorating stores.

Fresh from the Farm

Why not serve a fresh-from-the-farm brunch with a centerpiece of organic eggs in all different shapes, sizes, and colors?

When plating dinners for tableside service, set up an assembly line in the kitchen and assign each helper a different task. Here, tastes of Alaskan salmon and halibut are prepared for presentation at a dinner in the Pacific Northwest.

Brighten a buffet with a cheery selection of ready-to-eat wrap sandwiches. To prepare, don't overfill wraps. Cut sandwiches in half then roll in sheets of patterned scrapbooking paper to add color and practicality to your table.

First courses don't always have to be served at the dining table. Arrange a tasting course for soups by the fire. Ladle through a funnel into individual shot glasses of soups, garnish with a drizzle of cream and smoked paprika, or top with spicy globe basil flowers or toasted almonds. Select your colors and textures to reflect the season. Incorporate one-of-a-kind serving pieces, like the pheasant pitcher and the feather ball. Add found treasures like the hickory branch, pinecones, and slivered nut shells to invite conversation.

"What really defines a great palate, I think, is taste memory. It has as much to do with your head as with your tongue. . . A well-developed taste memory comes with experience and the willingness to try new flavors."
— Andrew Knowlton

Scotch Tasting

TIP

A proper tasting will include nosing glasses, distilled water, and soda crackers to cleanse the palate between sips.

When enjoying an event like a wine tasting or single malt scotch tasting, set up tasting stations around the house with plenty of fresh glasses.

A bridal shower or engagement party can be every bit as elegant as a wedding – with minimal cost and effort. The table is set up along a garden path where blooms are lush and the setting evokes a romantic theme. Beverages are served in a cut-glass punch bowl. To achieve the dramatic look of a tiered wedding cake, assemble cakes of similar color and design on escalating tiers. Here, crystal risers were used to add continuity, and bunches of fresh flowers at the highest peak and on each of the cakes repeat the color theme on the entire arrangement.

Vintage lace adds the perfect touch of history, while embroidered handkerchiefs collected over the years serve as napkins.

Lemonade Days

Fresh yellow and white is the perfect combination for a summer afternoon sweets party. Build a theme with like-colored desserts arranged on similar serving pieces. Here, lemon treats are grouped in lovely display.

Far left:
Get ready for guests with glasses rimmed with lemon wheels and a dish of old-fashioned sugar cubes.

Left:
Petit fours and lemon tarts are the perfect bite-sized treats.

Tuck fresh blooms throughout the buffet for a casual, refreshing look.

Exploring Color

Drama can be achieved in many ways, but one simple way to punch up the power of a meal is by focusing on a single color for maximum impact.

Clementines become the perfect serving bowls for tiny scoops of orange blossom sorbet. Simply hollow out the fruit and use varying sizes of melon ballers to create visual interest in this dessert display. Top each mound with slivers of orange peel. Freeze until serving time. I took advantage of a Chinese porcelain plate with an orange and white chrysanthemum pattern. Since I was unsure of this plate's acceptability for food, I layered over it a rounded-edge glass plate. The pattern was still prominent, and my table presentation reflected a variety of orange hues.

The new neutral is delicious. Simple olive oil and herb pasta is portioned for individual diners in sleek glasses. To serve, arrange on a platter covered with semolina flour. Drag a cake comb through the flour to create an added visual and textural dimension to your presentation.

Bluetinis with lime cube skewers look cool and oceanic on a tray of soft-hued sea glass.

"We should look for someone to eat and drink with before looking for something to eat and drink..."

— Epicurus

Take guests to the beach with a whitewashed display of crab salad. Scallop shells (gathered from beachcombing trips to Dog Island) make the perfect hand-held individual serving bowls. Fill a serving tray with a "sandy" layer of toasted breadcrumbs then nestle shells. Intersperse sprigs of fresh dill and found treasures to finish the seaside scene.

Guacamole and tortilla diamonds blend perfectly with this pale green serving duo.

An emerald green serving platter is dressed with sugar snap peas, snow peas, pea tendrils, and, for crunch, wasabi coated dried peas.

Red and white transferware dishes create a beautiful table when combined with more contemporary red glass pieces and amazing toile table linens. Add plenty of candles and the ruby tones will sparkle all night. But don't be in a rush to buy flowers. A few snips of greenery from your yard will dress your table in a natural beauty that puts guests at ease.

When serving foods of uniform color, go for contrast in the presentation. Here, creamy corn soup takes center stage in solid black bowls. If this soup were served in a white bowl, the effect would be pale. While a monochrome palette can be elegant, diners' appetites will be stimulated by a more vibrant presentation.

"After dinner sit a while, and after supper walk a mile."

— English Saying

Summer Fun

Dinner on the deck gets dressed up for a party with the addition of colorful paper lanterns. The dollar store is a great place to pick up party supplies and make your table more festive. These lanterns come two to a package and fold flat for easy storage.

Give guests a visual feast at the table's center and keep arrangements low enough that sight lines are not obstructed. Here, fresh greens are interspersed with limes and hydrangea blooms. Varying heights, shapes, and colors of candles makes for an artistic interpretation of the traditional floral centerpiece.

TIP

Citrus fruits can work double duty as place cards. Simply write guests' names on cards, affix cards to a toothpick, and insert into fruit. Set at each place setting for a fanciful, scented addition to the summer table.

Color plays such an important role in food presentation. Here, cheerful plates contrast beautifully with the spring green floral placemats. The crisp white embroidered napkin is tied with curling ribbon and accented by a few sprigs of purple statice.

Create a signature cocktail to honor an occasion. Here, muddled limes and superfine sugar are topped by chilled vodka and crushed ice. Grandmother's vintage crystal glasses can add an unexpected touch of luxury to an outdoor setting.

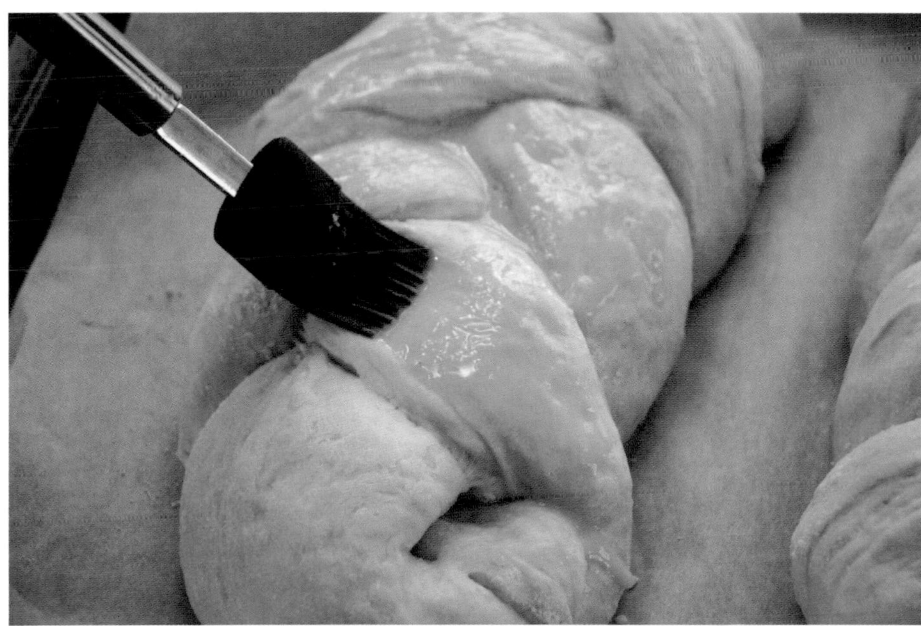

Instead of baking your bread in a simple loaf pan, experiment with shape and form. This challah bread is fashioned traditionally in a braid. To achieve a glossy, golden finish on the bread, it is brushed with an egg yolk and water wash, allowed to dry, then brushed again with the mixture before baking. The silicone head of the pastry brush allows for easy cleanup.

"I am going to learn to make bread tomorrow. So you may imagine me with my sleeves rolled up, mixing flour, milk, saleratus, etc., with a deal of grace. I advise you if you don't know how to make the staff of life to learn with dispatch."

—Emily Dickinson

"...the best poet is the man who delivers our daily bread: the local baker...."

— Pablo Neruda

Challah and other breads can also be rolled into a long loaf, coiled, and baked "turban" style in a rising circle shape. If you are not a baker, don't let it stop you from baking beautiful breads. Commercially prepared bread dough, available in both the dairy case and the freezer section of your local grocery, can be fancifully shaped to beautiful effect.

Grocery store bakeries feature bagged bake-and-eat breads. These partially cooked loaves are perfect for refining to suit your personal taste. Pick and clean sprigs of your favorite fresh herbs, beat one egg with a few teaspoons of water, and use a pastry brush to baste the herbs to the bread with the egg wash. Bake as directed. The loaves will come out of the oven golden and fragrant and will make a week-night meal just a little more special.

"Good bread is the most fundamentally satisfying of all foods; good bread with fresh butter, the greatest of feasts!"

— James Beard

Quick Garnishes and Wow Tips

Explore the beauty of fresh citrus slices set against glass.

High Impact Presentation

The reality of today's busy schedules is that some days, the cook's schedule is just too chaotic to plan an elegant presentation for every food prepared. If you only have time to do one something special, keep these simple presentation techniques in mind to add a jolt of impact to your table.

Toasted nuts add crunch and texture to a meal. To perfectly toast nuts, heat a dry pan on medium, add nuts and toss gently every minute or so until nuts begin to brown. The natural oils in the nuts will be enough to prevent sticking. Watch carefully to prevent burning. Remove to a paper towel and salt if desired. Toasted nuts may be frozen in airtight bags for later use.

Accent freshly grilled Asian-flavored meats with a stand of specialty mushrooms and fresh ginger root. When service time is over, loosely cover the mushrooms and refrigerate. When ready to cook, rinse the mushrooms and sauté in sesame oil and garlic for an exotic side dish to your next meal.

Investigate new and different drinks to serve your guests, like this luscious Italian wild strawberry liqueur. In honor of my grandparents, I dressed the table with French lace from my wedding and make a toast in their 50th anniversary glasses.

A vintage cutwork plate is the perfect foil for the artistic character of sliced heirloom tomatoes. Dress with cracked black pepper, a drizzle of extra virgin olive oil, and a sprig of sweet basil for a tasty first of the season salad.

"It's difficult to think anything but pleasant thoughts while eating a homegrown tomato."

— Lewis Grizzard

Top right:
Transfer slow-roasted campari tomatoes to a basil-lined gratin dish for help-yourself dinner service. Tomato juices mix with olive oil and fresh herbs for a flavor-rich sauce for the orecchiette "little ears" pasta with crumbled bacon.

Right:
Bow to tradition – Italian tradition, that is. Hard salty cheeses like parmesan Reggiano and piave vecchio are often served drizzled with fresh honey at serving time

To present gifts of your home-baked cookies, purchase small jars and colorful ribbon. Cut circles of parchment slightly smaller than width of jar. Layer cookies with parchment circles, seal jar and adorn with ribbon.

Corn is an all-time barbecue favorite, but here's an idea to wake it up. Boil corn until just crisp-tender then pan roast in brown butter seasoned with a smoked paprika and ancho chili powder. Rewrap corn in husks (silks removed) and tie for a handy buffet presentation. Corn can be prepared in advance and kept warm on a baking sheet in a 200-degree oven.

A traditional party favorite is a layered Mexican-inspired dip. Why not create individual servings as a first course? To achieve this tri-colored treat, pan-crisp triangles of flour tortillas and layer with black beans, sliced olives, fresh tomatoes, cheese, and sour cream.

Radish roses are traditional, but you can certainly have more fun. Using a bird's eye knife or other sharp blade, go with your imagination and carve initials, hearts, stripes, and abstract designs into the radishes. Plunge carved veggies into ice water until ready to use, and serve with plenty of salt and fresh butter. These are served on a rubberwood platter, which is an eco-friendly newcomer in the sustainable wood market.

Sometimes you just need to shake up the dinnertime routine with a wacky place setting. Here, a funny-faced pop art picture of my nephew Daniel becomes a place card in a jar of gumballs and fruit ropes. Kids love surprises – like the candy straw and the pipe cleaner butterflies. Just be sure they wait until after dinner to enjoy the props!

"The first of all considerations is that our meals shall be fun as well as fuel."

— Andre Simon

A slice of cake, a few lifesavers, and three magic wishes make a child's after-dinner treat into an event to remember.

Summer's mammoth basil leaves are the perfect base for prosciutto, fresh mozzarella, and wedges of campari tomatoes. Serve open-faced and encourage guests to wrap leaves around filling to eat.

You don't always need flowers to make a creative centerpiece. Here, sprigs of fresh sage, sweet basil, German thyme, lemon thyme, mint, and lemon balm are tied with kitchen twine. Arrange one mini bouquet at each guest's place setting for a fragrant addition to your table that can later be used to prepare another meal.

A perfectly brewed cappuccino needs no adornment other than the daily paper and a nice view to the outside world.

Even non-alcoholic drinks can look beautiful. Here, sparkling French lemonade is layered with tones of pink and red. A teaspoon of maraschino cherry juice and a single cherry are dropped in to anchor the drink; their weight causes them to settle at the bottom and allows the top layer of the drink to remain pale pink and effervescent.

A trip to the dollar store netted these brightly-colored takeout boxes. Wash thoroughly and arrange with a luncheon salad for a fun tabletop presentation.

"The more you eat, the less flavor; the less you eat, the more flavor."

— Chinese proverb

Serve up old-fashioned home fries in a rolled paper bag. Here, a trio of seasonings offers the diner delectable choices.

A classic after-dinner drink is the illustrious Irish coffee, dense with heavy whipping cream, Irish whiskey, and a dash of crème de menthe. Serve in slender coffee mugs that allow the richness of the drink to remain on display, and offer guests swizzle sticks of old-fashioned rock candy.

Veggies can be fun for the kids. Broccoli marinated in shimmering raspberry walnut dressing takes the shape of a holiday tree, adorned by cherry tomato ornaments. Consider adding garlands of thinly sliced yellow pepper. Use a slotted spoon to serve.

"May your home always be too small to hold all your friends."

— Irish toast

Make breakfast for the kids more fun by serving eggs in a funny bowl. This retired candy dish gives scrambled eggs a reason to cluck.

Kids can't resist treats served in their favorite toys. These "baby dogs" are a great handheld snack to enjoy while building blocks. Use flying discs in place of plates for an added bit of whimsy.

Kids' parties are an open invitation to have fun. Here, a racetrack serves up candies, while colorful snack cups dish out goodies in kid-friendly portions.

A vintage egg dish has many uses besides displaying hard boiled eggs. Consider using the compartmentalized piece for serving truffles, stuffed cherry tomatoes, filled new potatoes, and other round treats. The oval depression is perfect for keeping these treats upright and easily accessible. Helpful hint: Chocolates allowed to rest at room temperature will have a higher sheen than those fresh from the refrigerator, like these truffles from a master chocolate maker.

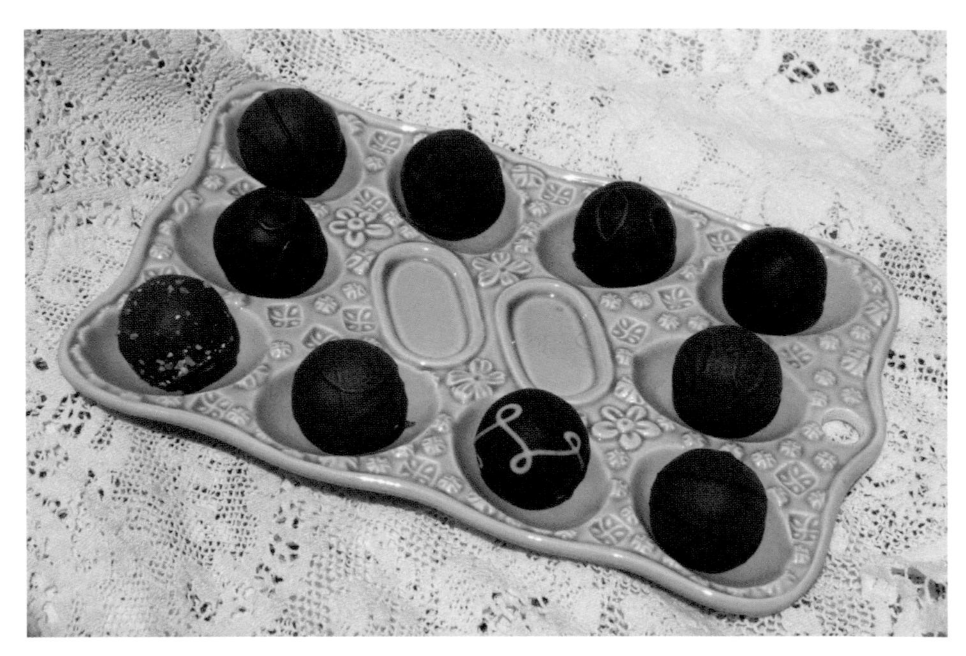

Big parties can be messy affairs with chip bowls spilling over onto tabletops. Package snack chips in individual parchment cones for grab-and-go convenience.

Sunset calls for a warming drink and a crisp wedge of citrus.

Table Settings

Dressing the table should be a delightful part of the food presentation process. By taking care to select the linens and the dishware, and by adding a personalized touch to individual place settings through flowers or hand-written notes, guests will be treated to an enhanced culinary experience.

A sunny day invites cheerful table settings. Layer plates, vary shapes, and complement with individual floral arrangements at each place.

Think outside the box when it comes to napkin rings. Here, natural-coated wire twists are topped with a fresh mushroom. Hand-written place cards are propped on a pair of mushrooms and a bed of moss.

Take breakfast outdoors with fresh-picked blooms, a crystal glass of juice, and grandma's china. Here, a sumptuous treat of buttery pancakes topped with caramelized bananas makes a fabulous meal. Puffy pancakes won't roll easily. Add an extra egg to the batter for a thinner, crepe-like result that browns quickly and rolls beautifully.

"At a dinner party one should eat wisely but not too well and talk well but not too wisely."

— W. Somerset Maugham

Before blooms completely fade away, give them new life by clipping stems short, arranging in shot glasses, and dressing up an everyday table setting.

The traditional formal place setting.

This giant candy house was made in the grand tradition of the pre-Civil War era homes in Frederick, Maryland. To achieve the look of age-dusted bricks, a cocoa icing base was applied to a cardboard house. The brick pattern was drawn by making subtle impressions in the icing with the tip of a knife. Before the icing dried, powdered sugar was gently blown onto the surface. Once the brick coat thoroughly dried, separately decorated windows and doors were applied with an extra dollop of royal icing. To complete the look, royal icing was piped between the wafer cookie roof and along the eaves. Though the surface is technically edible, it's probably best to simply admire your creation.

TIP

Explore your food creativity on mini edible canvases. Purchase or bake gingerbread cookies and use tubes of decorator icing to create patterns, small pictures, and monograms. Perfect to use as place cards!

Your Cooking Resource Guide

To help you on your quest to become a better cook and to learn more about techniques mentioned, consider some of my personal favorite outstanding culinary volumes. This list is by no means comprehensive but will give you an excellent starting point to build your own cooking library. Newer editions of some books may be available. Enjoy!

Michelle Valigursky

Great Cooking Reference Books

Herbst, Sharon Tyler. ***Food Lover's Companion,*** Second Edition. Barron's Cooking Guide, 1995.Comprehensive definitions of over 4,000 food, wine, and culinary terms.

Hemphill, Ian. ***The Spice and Herb Bible,*** Second Edition. Robert Rose, Inc., 2006.

Joachin, David. ***The Food Substitutions Bible.*** Robert Rose, Inc., 2005. More than 5,000 substitutions for ingredients, equipment, and techniques.

Norman, Jill, editor-in-chief. ***The Cook's Book.*** DK Publishing, Inc., 2005. Techniques and tips from the world's master chefs.

Peterson, James. ***What's a Cook to Do?*** Artisan, 2007. An illustrated guide to 484 essential tools, tips, techniques, and tricks.

Riely, Elizabeth. ***The Chef's Companion: A Culinary Dictionary,*** Third Edition. John Wiley and Sons, Inc., 2003. The indispensable guide to over 5,000 culinary terms.

Willan, Anne. ***La Varenne Pratique***, Crown Publishers, Inc., 1989. The complete illustrated cooking course: techniques, ingredients, and tools of classic modern cuisine with more than 2,500 full-color photographs.

Cookbooks for Beginning Cooks

Coulson, Zoe. ***The Good Housekeeping Illustrated Cookbook***. Hearst Books, 1980.

Garten, Ina. ***The Barefoot Contessa Cookbook***. Clarkson Potter/Publishers, 1999.

Becker, Ethan, Becker Rombauer, Marion, and Rombauer, Irma. ***Joy of Cooking, 75th Anniversary Edition.*** Scribner, 2006.

Peterson, James. ***Vegetables.*** William Morrow and Company, Inc., 1998.

Stewart, Martha. ***Martha Stewart's Quick Cook Menus***. Clarkson N. Potter Inc., Publishers, 1988. Fifty-two meals you can make in under an hour.

Cookbooks for Curious Cooks

Bastianich, Lidia. ***Lidia's Italy.*** Alfred A. Knopf, 2007.
Beranbaum, Rose Levy. ***The Cake Bible.*** William Morrow and Company, Inc., 1988.
Beranbaum, Rose Levy. ***The Pie and Pastry Bible.*** Scribner, 1998.
Claiborne, Craig. ***The New York Times Cookbook,*** Revised Edition. William Morrow Cookbooks, 1990.
Florence, Tyler. ***Tyler's Ultimate.*** Clarkson Potter/Publishers, 2006.
Jaffrey, Madhur. ***World Vegetarian.*** Clarkson N. Potter, 1999.
Valigursky, Michelle and Dumon, Marilyn. ***The Holiday Feast***. Continental Cooks Publishing, 1991.
Valigursky, Michelle. ***Pasta Pronto!*** Barrington Books, 1993.

Cookbooks for Advanced Cooks

Beck, Simone and Child, Julia. ***Mastering the Art of French Cooking, Volumes 1 and 2.*** Alfred A. Knopf, 1983 and 2001. Includes recipes for mastering every sauce you'd ever want to make.
Colicchio, Tom. ***Craft of Cooking.*** Clarkson Potter/Publishers, 2003
Desaulniers, Marcel. ***Death by Chocolate: The Last Word on a Consuming Passion.*** Rizzoli, 2003.
Desaulniers, Marcel. ***The Trellis Cookbook.*** Simon and Schuster, 1992.
Pasternack, David and Levine, Ed. ***The Young Man & the Sea.*** Artisan, 2007.

Websites with How-To Cooking Videos

www.foodnetwork.com
www.gourmandia.com
www.lookandtaste.com
www.rouxbe.com

Websites with Reader-Submitted Recipes

www.allrecipes.com. Includes readers' ratings.
www.cooks.com

Websites with Adventurous Recipes

www.epicurious.com
www.kraftfoodscompany.com. Great resource for kids' ideas.
www.southernliving.com
www.michellecooks.com. Your inspirational source for ideas to help you cook and entertain more creatively!

Index

A well-organized pantry makes preparing to present food beautifully a pleasure.

Other Schiffer Books

www.schifferbooks.com

Table Decoration: with Fruits and Vegetables. Angkana and Alex Neumayer. The art of fruit and vegetable carving has its roots in Asia, but today the creation of edible decorations is popular worldwide. Learn to create remarkable decorations for the table and garnishes for glasses and plates. Many tips, 440 color photos, patterns, and practical, step-by-step directions guide you through little works of art that are easy to produce. Carve a flower, shape a fish, a bell, the sun and moon. You will be adding light touches to your meals from here forward.
Size: 8 1/2" x 11" • 440 color photos • 128 pp.
ISBN: 978-0-7643-3510-5 • hard cover • $24.99

Table Decor. E. Ashley Rooney. We all know how to set tables, but do we know how to make them beautiful? With this book, you can realize the magic of table decor. With over 300 color illustrations and many practical and inventive solutions, this book covers the table, from soup to nuts or gardens to dining rooms, and many places in between. This book acquaints you with the charm of table décor, whether it is traditional, romantic, modern, or simple. The decorators featured are both professional and gifted, from many diverse backgrounds, and working in dozens of styles. There are ideas for every occasion and taste. By keeping the focus on texture, color, simple containers, and lots of ordinary household items, you can turn a simple meal into something fabulous by varying the items you use together. Here you will find the inspiration to create table settings with style, using your own china and silverware. See how designers and decorators mix, experiment, and create table décor with modern accouterments or pair antiques with new, ornate, or simple.
Size: 8 1/2" x 11" • 511 color photos • Index • 128 pp.
ISBN: 0-7643-2472-1 • soft cover • $24.95

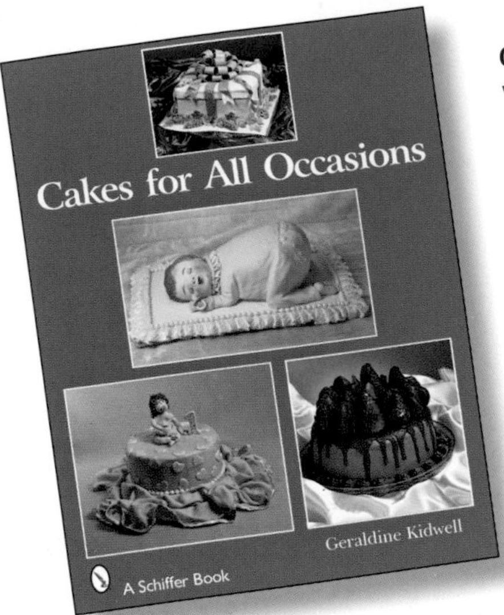

Cakes For All Occasions. Geraldine Kidwell. Learn to create 18 beautiful decorated cakes with a leading master at your elbow, coaching you from start to presentation. Specialty cakes for children, teens, weddings, holidays, and special celebrations can be made with these sequential instructions and over 330 color photographs of each step. Useful patterns will help get you started, and the cake recipes and list of suppliers will inspire you for years to come. The instructions are carefully designed for beginners, and words of encouragement throughout give you the confidence to complete a fantastic result each time. You will want to make and decorate another cake right away.
Size: 8 1/2" x 11" • 334 color photos • 112 pp.
ISBN: 978-0-7643-2904-3 • soft cover • $24.95

Sugar Art. Geraldine Kidwell and Barbara Green. The worlds of sugar art and cake decorating come together in this new how-to book. Both decorative panorama egg and sugar moldings appear in 371 color images. Whether a homemaker or a professional decorator, you'll marvel at ways to add a seasonal touch to your creations. Includes step-by-step directions for 15 cake designs for a baby shower, June bride, fruitful harvest, and more. See how a little sugar can provide an artistic element to your cake, home, or office.
Size: 8 1/2" x 11" • 371 color images • 128 pp.
ISBN: 978-0-7643-3382-8 • soft cover • $24.99

Entertaining with Flowers: The Floral Artistry of Bill Murphy. Bill Murphy. Floral designer Bill Murphy strives to create an enchanted experience for every event he designs. Join him as he lavishes a spring bridal shower, a tropical dinner party, a garden party, retirement celebration, and weddings winter, spring, summer and fall. Murphy illustrates step-by-step how he creates some of his charming illusions — dew drop beading on foliage, folded display napkins, and his signature candle-lit crystal displays.
Size: 11" x 8-1/2" • 235 color photos • 112 pp.
ISBN: 0-7643-2556-6 • hard cover • $29.95

Creating Floral Centerpieces. Bill Murphy. Join professional floral designer Bill Murphy, AIFD, to learn a florist's essential skills. Murphy explains step-by-step the creation of more than 25 impressive floral displays, from charger plates and napkin rings to kettle-sized, exotic centerpieces that will take your breath away. From basic bouquet tying skills through techniques using wire and floral adhesive, you will be inspired to adorn every event with flowery creations. Detailed photos will help you develop the confidence you need to branch out on your own, amazing friends and family with artful creations.
Size: 8 1/2" x 11 • 288 color photos • 112 pp.
ISBN: 978-0-7643-3459-7 • hard cover • $29.99

Schiffer books may be ordered from your local bookstore, or they may be ordered directly from the publisher by writing to:
Schiffer Publishing, Ltd.
4880 Lower Valley Rd.
Atglen, PA 19310
(610) 593-1777; Fax (610) 593-2002
E-mail: Info@schifferbooks.com

Please visit our web site catalog at *www.schifferbooks.com* or write for a free catalog. Please include $5.00 for shipping and handling for the first two books and $2.00 for each additional book. Full-price orders over $150 are shipped free in the U.S.

Printed in China